DINOSAUR DESTINATIONS

Finding America's Best Dinosaur Dig Sites, Museums & Exhibits

Jon Kramer, Julie Martinez and Vernon Morris

Adventure Publications
Cambridge, Minnesota

Photo Credits

Unless otherwise noted, all photos from the authors or royalty-free stock photography sites. Many thanks to the following people and organizations for use of their photos in this book.

18, Bureau of Land Management **22**, Fred McWilson; model by Guy Darrough (www.lostworldstudios.com) **23**, Smithsonian Institution National Museum of Natural History **26**, James St. John (Geology, Ohio State University at Newark) **27**, James St. John (Geology, Ohio State University at Newark) **28**, New England At-Hand guide app–Robert Gray **29**, New England At-Hand guide app–Robert Gray **32**, M-NCPPC **38**, Daderot, Wikimedia Commons **44**, Great Plains Dinosaur Museum **46**, Released into Public Domain by Wikipedia User Smallbones **47**, Released into Public Domain by Wikipedia User Smallbones **49**, Nash Dinosaur Track Quarry and Rock Shop **50**, PaleoAdventures **51**, PaleoAdventures **58**, Bureau of Land Management **59**, Bureau of Land Management **64**, Two Medicine Dinosaur Center **66**, Ben Townsend **67**, Ben Townsend **132**, Released into public domain by Wikipedia user Ammodramus **133**, Released into public domain by Wikipedia user Ammodramus **134**, Sara Feldt, NPS **137**, Alisha Vargas **139**, NPS Photo **140**, NPS Photo **145**, NPS Photo **148**, Kevin Saff **152**, Larry D. Moore

Edited by Brett Ortler and Sandy Livoti
Cover and book design by Lora Westberg

Copyright 2016 by Jon Kramer
Published by Adventure Publications
820 Cleveland Street South
Cambridge, Minnesota 55008
1-800-678-7006
www.adventurepublications.net
All rights reserved
Printed in China
ISBN: 978-1-59193-517-9

DINOSAUR
DESTINATIONS

Finding America's Best Dinosaur Dig Sites, Museums & Exhibits

Acknowledgments

It takes a lot of grit, muscle, dedication, and patience to dig dinosaurs and it helps to have companions to share the load. There are many people who were instrumental in making it happen for us:

We never used his first name—it was always **Mr. Shimizu.** He came into our world at the exact right time, facilitating our jump into the world of dinosaurs. His enthusiasm and financial support were vital, and we are grateful for his patronage.

If not for **Jeff Parker**, the story of Potomac Museum Group's dinosaur digging in Wyoming would have been quite different and certainly not as remarkable as it was. Jeff provided us with immensely valuable assistance in many forms and, in his typical magnanimous nature, asked for little in return. Your kind-nesses are appreciated and have been passed on to the next generation.

Bruce Erickson of the Science Museum of Minnesota has been a wise mentor and invaluable support-er of all our research efforts—dinosaurian and otherwise. Through your encouragement we have seen more deeply into the past and the present. It has enriched us all.

Bill Mason! You know who you are, and many more people need to as well. Bill has supplied the glue that holds it all together, both literally, through his company PaleoBond, and figuratively, through his unending generosity.

Our late friends **Jack Marchant** and his mother **Marjorie** opened their ranch and home to us for many memorable years. We'll always remember the wild laugh and high hellos from Jack as he came riding up over the ridge with his dog Mary Jane jumping all over him as he visited us in camp each evening.

Once upon a time there was an educational and research company called **Potomac Museum Group**. It was a bold endeavor that is now fading and fossilizing in its own unique way. In addition to my fantastic business partner **Hal Halvorson**—who was an inspiring companion and intrepid field director —there were many employees of PMG who proved invaluable in digging dinosaurs with us. They helped shape the lives of hundreds of school kids and educators. These folks were generally underpaid and over-worked but endured harsh conditions with a smile. **Kent Cooper** was a particularly valuable asset to us all and a great camp director. Some of the other outstanding supporters are (in alphabetical order only): **Clayton Black, Ray Colby, Janine Halvorson, Kathleen Heaney, Wendy Kimmer, Kirk Leavesley, Julie Martinez, Mike McAneney, Vern Morris, Jennifer Pawlson, Jennifer Wickland.** Others were: **Calista, Camille, George, Jeff,** a few **Joes, Kate, Katie, Matt, Mike, Paul, Ryoichi,** a couple

Sashas, and several **Toms**. There are undoubtedly others whose names are not here and I take the blame for that. But be it resolved that we fully appreciate all who helped dig up ancient histories that created lasting memories.

Those were the dirty companions of digging. Now it's time to call out those who helped get this little book off the ground—or out of the ground, so to speak: First among these is our editor **Brett Ortler**, who has been more than just "instrumental" in this creation—he's been a singular champion of this entire enterprise. Indeed, the idea originated with him and for that we are happily indebted. It's been a fun time digging up dinosaurs and memories with Brett! Sometime we might even take him along to dig up old bones—he certainly deserves that, at least!

How can we thank **Gordon** and **Gerri Slabaugh** for their encouragement and help over the years? What a ride it's been! The many books we've worked on together have enriched us so much more than we could have imagined. The two of you will always have a place in our hearts. We'll miss your wit, wisdom and smiles at work on future books but will look for you in the wild adventures ahead.

Contents

Introduction

A Decade Digging Dinosaurs

During the 1980s my friend Hal and I took a right turn and ended up 280 million years back in time. We were tracking an elusive lizard that had left footprints in the giant sand dunes that eventually became the Coconino sandstone of Arizona. By the end of the day we had collected evidence aplenty and the game was afoot. Over the next two decades we returned to the same area again and again to carry on the hunt. But we never found anything more than tracks and traces. Eventually our small company, Potomac Museum Group, collected hundreds of specimens of fossil trackways and brought them back to the Twin Cities for study. (We donated the collection to the Science Museum of Minnesota several years ago). Although these fossils predate dinosaurs by many millions of years, they hold important clues to evolution of both reptiles and mammals. One can learn a lot about animal structure and behavior by studying the tracks and traces they leave behind. We may not have found any bones, but our research was shedding new light on early reptile behavior.

As it happened, we had a retired Japanese friend who took a keen interest in our fossil research and would visit us daily as we cleaned, studied and documented our discoveries. Having a medical background, Mr. Shimizu was, naturally, more interested in bones than footprints and formulated an idea for a research project centered on dinosaurs, as it's well known that one can learn a lot about an animal from its bones. The only problem was that Mr. Shimizu didn't have any bones to study, and museums were not parting with any.

One day while touring our lab, he asked us, "Can you find dinosaur bones for me to study?" Up until that point we'd not really thought about looking for dinosaurs. Sure, they're sexy and all that, but they are big and very costly to collect, not to mention storing the finds and cleaning and mounting the bones. Still, we had enough experience in the field to know that given enough time and funding we could, without doubt, locate a dinosaur site. "Perhaps we can help each other out," Shimizu suggested. "*Suppose I bankroll your expeditions and donate to your research?*"

That sort of talk is music to the ears of any paleontologist!

So began our search. It eventually led us to a site in the high desert of Wyoming where, for ten years, we carried out the toilsome and rewarding ritual of digging dinosaurs all summer long. We excavated over

12 tons of bones, nearly all of which went to museums around the globe. Twelve tons might sound like a lot, but dinosaur bones are big and heavy and when you compare our effort to the over 700,000 tons dug out of Dinosaur National Monument, well that's just a drop in the old dinosaurian bucket. Still, it was enough for Mr. Shimizu and may have been for us as well. Well, maybe . . .

We had no clue what we were getting into when Mr. Shimizu made his bold offer, but it became, above all, a very rewarding educational experience, one that we shared with hundreds of school kids and science teachers who joined us at our site. There was, for example, the time we found an *Edmontosaurus* tail bone that had been broken and healed twice in the animal's lifetime. Then there was the discovery of tooth marks on some of the *Triceratops* bones, suggesting predation. And then we found a broken-off tooth embedded in a hadrosaur backbone . . . well, I could go on and on.

The point is dinosaurs are compelling in many ways. They've been super-charging the imagination of people for hundreds —even thousands—of years. From our perspective this is a very good thing and one that we'd like to pass on to you. This has inspired our modest effort here.

We hope that this little book of ours will not only help you to appreciate the magnificence, splendor, and awe of dinosaurs, but will also encourage and enable you to dig deeper into them, both figuratively and literally.

So get out there and dig those dinos! But if you choose to do it in the literal sense, please do so alongside a professional. Paleontologists need your help. And if you do end up discovering the find of a lifetime, drop us a line and let us know about it.

About Dinosaurs

Nothing fires up the imagination quite like dinosaurs—and there are over a thousand good reasons for that!

Dinosaurs are a hugely diverse group of animals that dominated the landscape from 230 million years ago up to the Cretaceous extinction event about 65 million years ago. Dinosaurs are known from every continent, including Antarctica. They were present in almost all climate zones and occupied nearly every terrestrial niche available to large animals through the middle and late Mesozoic. There are over 1,000 species of dinosaurs known today and that total keeps climbing as new discoveries are made each year.

Although the word dinosaur means "terrible lizard," dinosaurs are not actually lizards. Instead, they are a separate group of reptiles that didn't exhibit all the characteristics we commonly associate with reptiles—such as the sprawling limb posture found in lizards today. What's more, many of the prehistoric animals that are popularly thought of as dinosaurs (such as the very lizardly *Dimetrodon* or huge marine reptiles such as the plesiosaurs) weren't actually dinosaurs and are not all that closely related to them.

Real dinosaurs were remarkably diverse. Many were bipedal (walked on two legs), while others were quadrupedal (walked on four legs). Some were even able to easily shift between these stances. Elaborate display structures, such as horns or crests, were common in many dinosaur groups, and some developed skeletal modifications such as bony armor and spines as well as reinforcing rods (called ossified tendon) that helped to strengthen their backbones. Humans are poorly developed in comparison.

Early researchers recognized that dinosaurs had at least some reptilian characteristics and therefore assumed them to be cold-blooded and anything but agile. In those days people could not fathom how such large beasts could stand, let alone move around. So, the accepted response was to make them stupid, sluggish, and cold-blooded. This was popularized by museum displays and exhibitions that featured large dinosaurs slogging through swamps and bogs. Modern research has shown conclusively that the old school of thought was patently incorrect. We now know that dinosaurs were very active animals with elevated metabolisms and numerous adaptations for social interaction. Evidence suggests that egg laying and nest building are traits shared by many—possibly all—dinosaurs.

But if they were so advanced and successful, why did dinosaurs go extinct? The short answer is—they didn't.

Birds are, in fact, the progeny of dinosaurs. Yes, that little sparrow flitting around the table at the sidewalk café is, for all intents and purposes, a living dinosaur. The fossil record indicates that birds evolved from theropod dinosaurs during the Jurassic Period. Ever since Robert Bakker published his aptly-named *The Dinosaur Heresies* in 1986—where he bucked the old-school conventional notions and put forth the idea that birds descended from dinosaurs—the passage of time (and subsequent research) have proven him correct in many respects. Much of *The Dinosaur Heresies* now represents the accepted truth in paleontological circles.

Today, there are over 10,000 living species of birds, making them the most diverse group of terrestrial vertebrates. Like their dinosaur ancestors, they too are present in almost all climate zones and occupy an astonishing variety of terrestrial niches, many of which were not even around during the Mesozoic. Birds are, therefore, a testament to the enduring legacy of dinosaurs.

The Geologic Time Scale

Although we as a species have overrun the Earth and adapted to every conceivable climate and ecosystem, geologically speaking, we're young pups and the time we've spent on Earth pales when compared to that of many other species, including dinosaurs. Modern humans have been around roughly 200,000 years so far; dinosaurs, on the other hand, were running around the Mesozoic Era for roughly 135 million years. If we count birds, which are also descendants, dinosaurs have been on Earth for more than 200 million years, about 1,000 times longer than we have.

It gets much deeper: The oldest dinosaurs made their appearance about 230 million years ago. The oldest evidence of animals came on the scene about 600 million years before now, and the earliest known living organisms are about 3.5 billion years old. The oldest rocks on Earth clock in at a little more than 4 billion years old. So, yeah, Earth has obviously been around for awhile. Most scientists agree that our planet formed about 4.5 billion years before the ball started dropping in Times Square on New Year's Eve.

To make sense of it all, natural science researchers have developed the Geologic Time Scale. Figuring all this out took a few centuries, but it's been worth it, because the time scale divides up Earth's timetable into recognizable divisions so we can all speak the same language when discussing prehistoric events. The borders between these time periods may be adjusted as new evidence comes to light, but the basic divisions remain valid, and they are incredibly useful because it allows the Earth's geology to serve as a sort of calendar. Learning the basics of this calendar is therefore pretty important when studying dinosaurs; knowing what types of rocks are near you will tell you what you're likely to find (or won't).

ERA	PERIOD	EPOCH	AGE (million yrs.)
CENOZOIC Age of Mammals	QUATERNARY	recent	
		Pleistocene	.01
			2
	NEOGENE	Pliocene	5
		Miocene	24
	PALEOGENE	Oligocene	37
		Eocene	58
		Paleocene	66
MESOZOIC Age of Reptiles	CRETACEOUS		144
	JURASSIC		208
	TRIASSIC		245
PALEOZOIC Age of Fishes	PERMIAN		286
	PENNSYLVANIAN		330
	MISSISSIPPIAN		360
	DEVONIAN		408
	SILURIAN		438
	ORDOVICIAN		505
	CAMBRIAN		570
PRECAMBRIAN			

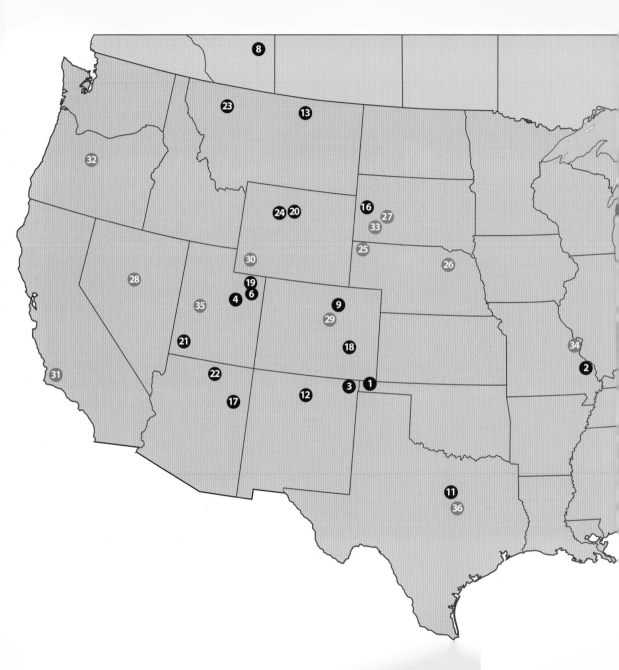

Fossil Site Map

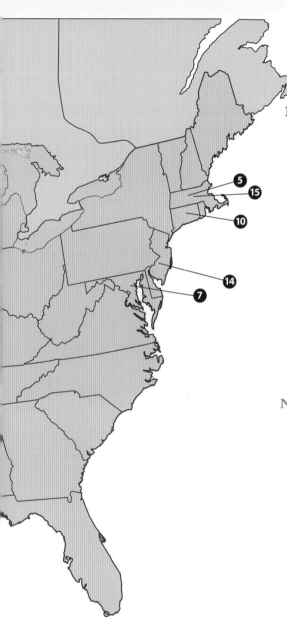

Dinosaur Fossil Sites:

1. Black Mesa Dinosaur Track Site

2. Bollinger County Museum of Natural History

3. Clayton Lake State Park

4. Cleveland Lloyd Dinosaur Quarry

5. Holyoke Dinosaur Footprints

6. Dinosaur National Monument

7. Dinosaur Park

8. Dinosaur Provincial Park

9. Dinosaur Ridge

10. Dinosaur State Park

11. Dinosaur Valley State Park

12. Ghost Ranch

13. Great Plains Dinosaur Museum

14. Haddonfield Dinosaur Site

15. Nash Dinosaur Track Site

16. PaleoAdventures

17. Petrified Forest National Park

18. Purgatoire River Dinosaur Track Site

19. Red Fleet State Park

20. Red Gulch Dinosaur Track Site

21. St. George Dinosaur Discovery Site at Johnson Farm

22. Tuba City Dinosaur Track Site

23. Two Medicine Dinosaur Center

24. Wyoming Dinosaur Center

Non-Dinosaur Fossil Sites:

25. Agate Fossil Beds National Monument

26. Ashfall Fossil Beds State Historical Park

27. Badlands National Park

28. Berlin-Ichthyosaur State Park

29. Florissant Fossil Beds National Monument

30. Fossil Butte National Monument

31. George Page Museum La Brea Tar Pits

32. John Day Fossil Beds National Monument

33. Mammoth Site of Hot Springs

34. Mastodon State Historic Site

35. U-Dig Fossils

36. Waco Mammoth National Monument

What to Know Before Fossil Collecting

Before you head out on a fossil hunt, you need to learn where you can and cannot collect fossils, as well as the types of fossils that are legal to collect where you are.

Fossil Hunting on Public Land

When it comes to fossil hunting, there's a big difference between public land and private land. Collecting fossils on public land is strictly regulated and sometimes outright banned altogether. What's more, collecting vertebrate fossils—fossils of animals with a backbone—on public land requires a permit. Vertebrate fossils are generally rarer than those of invertebrates, and without proper documentation of the discovery site, the fossils lose much of their scientific value. For this reason, permits are only granted to professional paleontologists. Long story short, you can't just go traipsing about on public land looking for dinosaurs or other vertebrate fossils. If you try it, you'll be heavily fined and could face jail time. There are, however, some opportunities to assist academic paleontologists in legal dinosaur hunts. Check with your local museum or university.

With that said, collecting invertebrate fossils (including petrified wood) is allowed on some public land, such as territory overseen by the Bureau of Land Management. But again, you need to know the rules where you're collecting, and just how much you can take home with you. Always check with local land managers.

Fossil Hunting on Private Land

The rules are different when it comes to private land. Collecting vertebrate and invertebrate fossils alike is allowed on privately owned land, as long as you have permission of the property owner. As you might expect, many private landowners charge a fee for the opportunity to dig for fossils, and some have even created entire businesses predicated on fossil digs. There are even organizations that allow you to participate in digs for dinosaurs. But don't expect to lug home an entire *Tyrannosaurus rex*. Ethical and reputable commercial ventures document their finds just as academic paleontologists do and sell or donate their finds to public institutions. This enables important fossils to be studied in perpetuity. Such a collaboration between researchers, commercial, and amateur paleontologists is essential, as there are far more amateur and commercial paleontologists in the field than academic paleontologists. These armies of enthusiastic and motivated weekend warriors help uncover many fossils that otherwise may go unnoticed.

When it comes down to it, the basics of responsible fossil collecting are fairly simple: Know where you are, know the rules, and above all else, put science before personal gain.

How to Use This Book

Written for the novice and the well-seasoned dinosaur hunter alike, this book includes four major sections.

Dinosaur Dig Sites, Dinosaur Tracks, Bone Beds and More (page 19)

If it's dinosaur dig sites you want, start here. This section includes everything from active dinosaur dig sites and preserved bone beds to famous dinosaur track sites where you can literally walk in the steps of dinosaurs. This section also includes a number of other sites, including museums and private ventures, which are well worth visiting for the dinosaur aficionado.

Each site description includes information about the site, the dinosaurs that once lived there, as well as what digging opportunities (if any) are available. Other dinosaur-related highlights are included as well. For example, at one site (page 48), you can purchase a real dinosaur track; at another (page 32) you can make your own plaster cast of a real dinosaur track and take it home with you! At some sites, you can even touch real dinosaur bones! To find out if there's a site near you, check out the site overview map on pages 14–15.

A Guide to Some of the Popular Dinosaurs of North America (page 68)

If you want to know more about the dinosaurs discussed in this book, flip no further! This section covers some of the famous dinosaurs found in North America, as well as some that you're probably not familiar with. Organized in a field-guide format, each account includes the basic details—the dino's length, weight and height—but it also features a wealth of additional information, including its former range (and a range map to see if it lived in your neck of the woods), the meaning of its name, fun facts, and more.

Non-Dinosaur Fossil Sites in North America (page 128)

So why would we include non-dinosaur species in this book? Well, many—including pterosaurs, plesiosaurs and ichthyosaurs—lived at the same time as dinosaurs and are often associated with them. Plus this allows us to highlight some of the other fascinating creatures that lived in North America, including the literal sea monsters and weird mammals that lived in North America after the dinosaurs went extinct—or not!—at the end of the Cretaceous.

A Guide to Some of the Popular Non-Dinosaur Fossil Species of North America (page 154)

From sea monsters, like plesiosaurus and mosasaurs, to lesser-known oddities like *Megatherium* (a giant sloth!), this section of the book is your guide to some strange non-dinosaur species of North America.

Dinosaur Dig Sites, Dinosaur Tracks, Bone Beds and More

North America wasn't the first place that dinosaurs were discovered, but the continent has been the site of some of the most famous and important dinosaur discoveries in the world. The following section highlights some of the finest North American dinosaur sites that are open to the public. When it comes to dinosaurs, we're cosmopolitan, so we've included everything from active dig sites and fossil track sites to former dig sites, public parks, and museums. Along the way, we've done our best to point out the best that each site has to offer, including unique opportunities, such as making your dinosaur track cast, sites that allow you touch a real dinosaur bone, and more. So get out there and start exploring!

Black Mesa Dinosaur Track Site

You might be thinking that because this site is way out in the boonies in Oklahoma, all you'll see is cows, grass, and cropland. But then you realize you're a dinosaur hunter and you don't really care what's on view *today*; it's what you can see from 100 million years ago that really counts. Located near Black Mesa, these famous dinosaur tracks have been preserved in sandstone next to Carrizo Creek. They were originally discovered in the 1980s, with a total of 47 footprints present. Unfortunately, many have weathered away, and only a third of the original tracks are visible today. The dinosaur tracks are located on private property, but happily, viewing them is allowed during daylight hours. (The above photo is from a professional photographer and was taken with permission.)

A Slip in the Mud

All dinosaur tracks are interesting, but a few of the tracks here have drawn scrutiny from scientists because they were deeper than the others and had unusual patterns. Puzzling out exactly what happened took some work, but the current consensus is that a dinosaur was walking in a muddy area and slipped, causing its foot to sink in more than in the other tracks. It's not clear what species left behind the track, but from the foot-print, it's a good bet that it was a theropod. Theropods are a large group of bipedal, carnivorous dinosaurs that included *Tyrannosaurus rex*, so just be glad you weren't here on the day the tracks were made.

When you visit the area, please remember that this is private property and respect the land and the tracks accordingly.

Gift Shop Finds: There is no gift shop here, but at nearby Black Mesa Preserve, you can bag something else. The preserve is home to the highest point in Oklahoma (4,973 feet), and this is a great way to introduce kids to "high-pointing," the somewhat random hobby of visiting the highest points in each state. It's a bit of an odd hobby, but it certainly is fun.

Location: Near Kenton, Oklahoma.

Type of Site: Dinosaur track site.

Age: 100 million years.

Site Rating: ★★★

Digging: No digging or collecting allowed.

For the Kids: See the gift shop note.

Also in the Area: Black Mesa State Park and Black Mesa Preserve are both nearby. The state park boasts camping and recreation opportunities, and the preserve protects over 1,600 acres of wild, rugged land.

Contact Info: This site is located in a remote area, so be sure to visit the website for detailed directions.

Site Details: www.travelok.com/listings/view.profile/id.2245

GPS: 36.938961 N, -102.960866 W

The site is remote, but seeing dinosaur tracks is almost always worth a drive!

Tracks during daylight hours

What's here?
Tracks from a bipedal, carnivorous dinosaur.

Bollinger County Museum of Natural History

Some people want dinosaurs, others want cows. In 1942 a geologist named Dan Stewart was working for the Missouri Geological Survey, looking for clay deposits in Bollinger County. One day he encountered a young boy who told him his family had found clay while digging on their property. This piqued Dan's attention. When he met the boy's mother, a Mrs. Chronister, she showed him something even more surprising: huge bones. Dan searched nearby and found more bones. In all, he found 14 tail bones, along with fragments of a few others. With permission, he had the bones examined by experts who identified them as belonging to a hadrosaur. Later, the Smithsonian Institution paid her a tidy sum of $50 for the bones, and she used the money to buy a cow. The Bollinger County Museum honors this discovery and features a full-size recreation of the find.

The Missouri State Dinosaur

Scientists originally thought the dinosaur found at this site was a sauropod (a plant-eating dinosaur). But additional research at the site in the 1980s indicated that it was actually a hadrosaur, a group of dinosaurs known informally as "duck-billed dinosaurs." More importantly the find represented a new species, which was labeled *Hypsibema missouriense*. The discoveries at the Chronister Dinosaur Site excited local paleontologists, and they soon became a point of pride for the entire county, even the whole state. You see, dinosaur finds are pretty rare in Missouri; in fact, *Hypsibema* was the first dinosaur discovered in the state. Since then, only a few fragments of other dinosaurs have been found. Realizing this, the local chamber of commerce decided to harness the dino-mania and branded the city as a paleontological must-see. As a result the Bollinger County Museum soon became a dino destination. It's well worth a trip, as it boasts a full-size replica of *Hypsibema*, a full floor of dinosaurs called the "Dinosaur Stampede," and geology and fossil exhibits. Also be sure to check out the museum's dinosaur egg incubator, a prop used in the third *Jurassic Park* movie.

Gift Shop Finds: The museum's gift store offers everything from minerals and fossils to T-shirts emblazoned with the state dinosaur's image.

The museum is also home to a 900-pound block of clay that was transported from the Chronister dinosaur site, so active research is often underway at the museum's fossil prep lab!

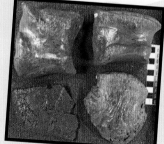

The original finds

Location: Marble Hill, Missouri.

Type of Site: Museum with a bone site nearby; the bone site is not yet open to public.

Age: 70 million years.

Site Rating: ★★★⯪

Digging: No digging or collecting.

For the Kids: You can actually touch and hold some of the items in the museum's geology room, including a variety of fossils!

Also in the Area: There are some interesting historic sites in the area. Bollinger Mill was first built in 1800 and burned down during the Civil War. It was rebuilt and still stands today.

Contact Info:
www.bcmnh.org/index.html

What's here?
A full-size replica of *Hypsibema missouriense* and lots of other dino fun.

Clayton Lake State Park

A hundred million years ago there was an infamous party here at Clayton Lake, one of which has gone down in Union County history. The funny thing is, no one would have been the wiser if telltale evidence hadn't been accidentally brought to light by a 1982 flood. Torrential rains swelled Clayton Lake to overflowing and washed over the earthen dam, scouring away sediment at the same time. When the waters receded, the townsfolk were aghast at what they saw: hundreds of footprints left by dinosaurian partygoers as they reveled in the mud-choked dance floor of the Mesozoic. The whole incident remains hush-hush to this day.

Dinosaur Freeway

The dinosaur tracks are one of the main attractions at this park and rightfully so, as about 500 tracks are found here. Most of them are from large herbivores, like *Hadrosaurus* (see page 104). Nonetheless, some tracks of large meat-eating theropod species are found here as well. The Clayton Lake track site is at the far end of what has been called the "Dinosaur Freeway," a once-muddy coastal region along the Western Interior Seaway, a body of water that split ancient North America in two during the Cretaceous. Such conditions were perfect to preserve tracks, and dinosaurs (among other animals) frequented the muddy shores. Other examples of the Dinosaur Freeway can be seen at Dinosaur Ridge on page 36.

Gift Shop Finds: There is no gift shop at the state park, so instead, take a hike! Capulin Volcano National Monument isn't all that far away from the park, and one of its trails leads to the bottom of the (extinct!) volcano's crater. It's not every day that you get to hike into a volcano!

Some scientists have suggested that the "Dinosaur Freeway" may have been a migration route!

A theropod track

What's here?
Tracks from hadrosaurs, iguanodons and theropods.

Location: Clayton, New Mexico.

Type of Site: A visitor center and excellent open-air track sites.

Age: 100 million years.

Site Rating: ★★★★

Digging: No digging or collecting. Self-guided and ranger-led interpretive hikes to tracks.

For the Kids: Clayton Lake is a great family recreational area.

Also in the Area: Nearby Capulin Volcano National Monument has many popular trails.

Contact Info:
Clayton Lake State Park: www.emnrd. state.nm.us/SPD/ claytonlakestatepark.html

Capulin Volcano National Monument: www.nps.gov/cavo

Cleveland Lloyd Dinosaur Quarry

ABOUT THE SITE Being at the top of the food chain isn't all that it's cracked up to be, especially if you were riding with the *Allosaurus* clan of central Utah during the Jurassic. What with all those other tribe members telling you what to do and your natural tendency to chase victims even if they are heading into a dangerous area, well, things can get a little dicey to say the least. And sometimes it doesn't turn out the way you plan. That's the situation one finds at Cleveland Lloyd Dinosaur Quarry, which just so happens to be the largest concentration of Jurassic dinosaur bones ever found. So what happened? The short version: A huge number of predatory dinosaurs appear to have been trapped in quicksand, which preserved their bones after they died.

Allosaurus Party

The Cleveland Lloyd Dinosaur Quarry is famous for a few reasons. First of all, more than 17,000 bones have been excavated here, with most now housed in the Utah Museum of Natural History. But they weren't any old bones, either. An incredible amount of *Allosaurus* bones were discovered, representing at least 46 individuals. Given that finding one individual dinosaur is a big deal, finding almost fifty is a bonanza. Best of all, there are plenty of dinosaurs left. Some of the deposit is now enclosed in a building that is open to the public.

Gift Shop Finds: There is no gift shop on-site, but if you're lucky, you can see paleontologists working on dinosaur excavations or fossil preparation, something you can't see just anywhere.

Location: Elmo, Utah.

Type of Site: A museum, and an enclosed bone site.

Age: 150 million years.

Site Rating: ★★★★★

Digging: No digging or collecting. Ranger-led interpretive hikes to fossil deposits.

For the Kids: Kids can participate in the BLM Junior Explorer Program.

Also in the Area: Just 10 miles away, Huntington State Park Recreational Area offers more than enough to keep you busy, including museums, boating, camping, mountain biking and hiking.

Contact Info: www.blm.gov/ut/st/en/fo/price/recreation/quarry.html

Be sure to check out the Butler Buildings, one of which is open to the public. There, visitors can see real dinosaur bones still in the ground!

These could do some damage . . .

What's here?

Allosaurus fossils are the most common, but a number of other dinos have been found here, including *Torvosaurus*, *Ceratosaurus*, *Stegosaurus*, *Brachiosaurus*, and *Camarasaurus*.

Holyoke Dinosaur Footprints

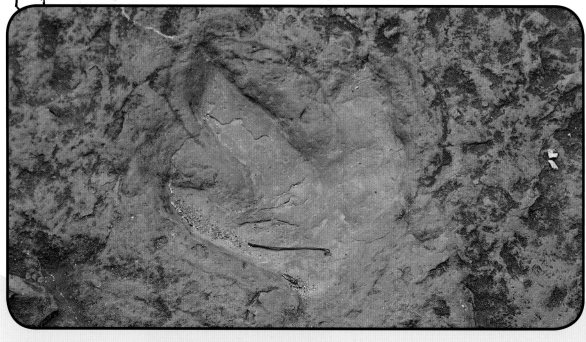

ABOUT THE SITE

It might be a little confusing that they simply named this place "Dinosaur Footprints," but the name is certainly accurate, as the site is home to a bounty of more than 130 dinosaur tracks. This site's famous dinosaur tracks first entered the limelight way back in 1838, when they were first scientifically documented. This was a pretty big deal, as these were the first dinosaur tracks to be formally described. So when you visit, you're not just walking along-side dinosaur tracks—if that isn't cool enough!—but you're also seeing an important part of dinosaur history, too.

The Name Doesn't Lie

When the tracks here were first discovered, dinosaur paleontology was in its infancy, but we've learned a lot about fossil tracks since then. The current consensus is that the tracks found here were made about 200 million years ago by as many as four distinct types of theropods (bipedal, carnivorous dinosaurs).

The site has more than just isolated footprints; many of the tracks are part of a series of tracks. There are more than twenty such trackways. Back in the mid to late 1800s, discovering a number of trackways was a major find because when dinosaurs were first discovered, it was commonly assumed they were oversized, solitary creatures. Finding many trackways in one place made it clear that these assumptions were wrong and that some dino species traveled in packs or groups.

Gift Shop Finds: There isn't a gift shop on-site, but the Children's Museum at Holyoke has a fine gift shop that features a variety of items pertaining to dinosaurs.

Can you imagine being the first scientist to realize that huge carnivorous beasts not only left their tracks behind, but that they also traveled in packs? Yikes!

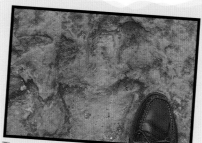

These tracks . . . aren't small

What's here?
Theropod tracks.

Location: Holyoke, Massachusetts.

Type of Dino Site: Historic dinosaur track site.

Age: 200 million years.

Site Rating: ★★★★

Digging: No digging or collecting.

For the Kids: The nearby Children's Museum at Holyoke provides a tot lot and hands-on activities for older children and is a great place for field trips and birthday parties.

Also in the Area: Wistariahurst is a historic former estate in Holyoke. It was built in 1848.

Contact Info:
Dinosaur Footprints: www.thetrustees.org/ places-to-visit/pioneer-valley/dinosaur-footprints. html
Children's Museum at Holyoke: www.childrens museumholyoke.org/

Dinosaur National Monument

The Carnegie Quarry is the main dinosaur attraction of Dinosaur National Monument, and it's easy to understand why: Thousands of dinosaur bones have been unearthed here, and many were shipped out to museums, including (not coincidentally) Pittsburgh's Carnegie Museum of Natural History. You might think there'd be nothing left after 700,000 tons of bones had been unearthed and carted off, but you'd be wrong! In fact, what is left is nothing short of breathtaking. The main attraction is the quarry's incredible display of bones, which fill a near-vertical wall and are in situ (still in the ground) inside the newly renovated building. There really is nothing like it anywhere else. The Monument has even more to offer: incredible hiking, camping, and rafting adventures, not to mention a rich cultural history, including some of the most famous ancient rock art on the continent.

A Week's Searching, then a Bonanza of Bones

Earl Douglass was no slacker. He knew how to buckle down and get on with the business of finding dinosaurs. Still, it wasn't easy or glamorous, especially in the hot, dusty nether-lands of Utah in 1909. Douglass had joined up with the Carnegie Museum of Pittsburgh some five years prior. In 1908, he and the director had located a few promising bones, and the museum had sent him back to see what else might be found. It only took him a week to find more. On August 17, while exploring a gulch not far from the previous year's site, he found a series of eight articulated tail bones of an *Apatosaurus* peeking out from the rock. The rest, as they say, was history, and the site soon produced thousands of amazing finds.

Gift Shop Finds: Want to take home a fossil? Well, you can't, but the gift shop offers the next-best thing: replica fossils of the dinosaurs found at the National Monument; examples include the bipedal predator *Allosaurus*, the large herbivore *Camarasaurus* and many others!

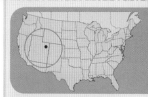

Location: Jensen, Utah.

Type of Dino Site: A museum with an enclosed bone bed.

Age: 149 million years.

Site Rating: ★★★★★

Digging: Dinosaur National Monument offers ranger-led hikes, but as of this printing, there are no digging opportunities.

For the Kids: The park participates in a number of programs for kids, including the Junior Ranger program, the Junior Cave Scientist program and other activities for kids.

Also in the Area: Visit nearby Vernal, Utah, to see some fabulous roadside dinosaur statues, one of which is a *T. rex* dressed up for various holidays.

Contact Info: www.nps.gov/dino/

Be sure to get a picture of yourself next to the huge fossil bones at the quarry.

The site actually allows you to touch some bones!

What's here?
Fossils of *Allosaurus, Apatosaurus, Camarasaurus, Diplodocus,* and *Stegosaurus.* You are even allowed to touch some of the real bones!

Dinosaur Park

The area looked a bit different 115 million years ago. It may straddle the Baltimore-Washington Parkway today, but back then there were dinosaurs stomping about and eating every gymnosperm in sight! The few bones and teeth they left behind were trapped in clay deposits of the Potomac Group, where some were preserved. Most clay deposits are pretty unremarkable and go unexplored—I've got some in my backyard pond if you want explore that—but these specific deposits were known as a source of iron, so they were in demand. While on the hunt for iron-rich clay, Phillip Tyson accidentally discovered two dinosaur teeth in 1858. His discovery was the first dinosaur find in Maryland, but it wasn't the last—the site continues to produce fossils, just 40 minutes from Washington, D.C.

Going Back 115 Million Years

The Dinosaur Park fossil area is fenced in and only open on the first and third Saturdays of each month (albeit year-round), but it's worth a visit, as spectators can join site paleontologists and volunteers in the search for fossils. Docents lead the way with demonstrations of screening for fossils in the sediment, all the while teaching students, young and not-so-young, about dinosaurs and paleontology.

Gift Shop Finds: There's no gift shop here, but one of the great benefits of this place is being not too far from Smithsonian National Museum of Natural History in downtown D.C. The Smithsonian is one of the greatest natural history museums in the world and a "must-see" for every true dinosaur hunter. It features a wide variety of dinosaurs from around the world. Unfortunately, the primary Dinosaur Hall is undergoing a long-term renovation that will not be completed until 2019. In the interim, dinosaur fossils, including *Tyrannosaurus rex* and *Triceratops* are on display in the Last American Dinosaurs exhibit on the museum's second floor; the exhibit runs until 2019.

Location: Laurel, Maryland.

Type of Dino Site: A small fossil site associated with Montpelier Mansion a few miles away.

Age: 115 million years.

Site Rating: ★★

Digging: There's no real digging to be had here, but kids can participate in the hunt for fossils by helping wash sediments/look for fossils.

For the Kids: The park offers two free fossil talks that are geared toward kids each month. It also operates a program where kids can help scientists wash sediments and look for fossils.

Also in the Area: The Smithsonian, enough said!

Contact Info: http://history.pgparks. com/sites_and_museums/ Dinosaur_Park.htm

Over the years, hundreds of fossils have been found by visitors during Dinosaur Park's open houses!

The Smithsonian

What's here?
Astrodon johnstoni. Clocking in at 50 or 60 feet long and 30 feet tall, *Astrodon* was a huge plant-eater.

Dinosaur Provincial Park

Dinosaur Provincial Park is one of the richest dinosaur locations on Earth. In addition to being one of Canada's provincial parks (like a "state park" in the U.S.), the location is even designated a UNESCO World Heritage site. What's all the fuss? Well, a whopping forty dinosaur species have been discovered at the park and more than 500 specimens have been unearthed and exhibited in museums around the globe. At several places in the park, there are untouched dinosaur bones literally sticking out of the ground.

Provincial Dinosaurs of Alberta

Dinosaur Provincial Park is located in a fairly remote area, but if you're a serious dinosaur hunter, this place is your Mecca. The first dinosaur skeletons discovered here were found in the 1880s. Since then, over 40 dinosaur species have been discovered and more than 150 complete skeletons have been unearthed, making it one of the richest dinosaur sites known. The specimens represent every known group of Cretaceous dinosaur, making it a veritable dinosaur zoo.

The park's tour programs allow visitors to see the dinosaurs up-close and personal. The Centrosaurus Quarry Hike, which is fairly demanding (not for kids younger than 7), brings visitors to a remote bone bed where hundreds of horned dinosaurs are entombed. Some of the bones here are simply jutting out of the surface. The tours at the park are popular, so be sure to reserve your tickets well in advance.

Gift Shop Finds: The park's gift shop features all sorts of items to remember your trip.

Location: Brooks, Alberta, Canada.

Type of Dino Site: A museum, exhibits and bone digs.

Age: 75 million years.

Site Rating: ★★★★★

Digging: The Fossil Safari Program is a hands-on program that lets you find and touch real fossils; it's perfect for families with children who love dinosaurs!

For the Kids: In addition to the dino activities, there are two performing art theaters that offer entertaining kids shows such as "Broadway in the Badlands."

Also in the Area: The park is only two hours from Calgary.

Contact Info:
www.albertaparks.ca/dinosaur.aspx

If you want to see fossils without going on a tour, visit one of the park's two Fossil Display Houses; one has a nearly complete hadrosaur skeleton, whereas the other has a full-size recreation of a dig site.

Raptors are just one of the many dinosaur groups found here

What's here?
Many dinosaur fossils, including *Centrosaurus*, *Styracosaurus*, *Pachyrhinosaurus*, *Chasmosaurus*, *Hadrosaurs*, *Corythosaurus*, *Lambeosaurus*, *Parasaurolophus*, and *Ankylosaurus*.

Dinosaur Ridge

Located on the western edge of the Denver metro area, Dinosaur Ridge features hundreds of dinosaur tracks, a small quarry of dinosaur bones, a visitor center, and interesting geological features. Hiking Dinosaur Ridge itself takes about 1–2 hours to see all of the sites (a total trek of about 2.5 miles). The site is one of the few places where visitors are allowed to touch exposed dinosaur bones. The bones may have belonged to *Stegosaurus* and *Apatosaurus*.

Road Construction is Great

You might grumble about work crews and detours adding travel time to your family vacation, but sometimes highway construction has its own rewards. Dinosaur Ridge is an example of the benefits. It probably would never have been discovered if it hadn't been accidentally unearthed during the construction of West Alameda Parkway in 1937. Unfortunately, in the early years, there were no specific laws to protect the site, so many tracks were vandalized and some were removed. Thankfully, things are different today, due in large part to the Friends of Dinosaur Ridge, a group dedicated to preserving, protecting, and educating the public about the site's unique scientific heritage.

Gift Shop Finds: Fossil replicas, great books, toys and T-shirts are all available at the visitor center.

Location: Morrison, Colorado.

Type of Site: A small museum with nearby dinosaur tracks and a bone bed.

Age: 165–75 million years.

Site Rating: ★★★↘

Digging: The site itself doesn't allow digging, but it does host field trips to interesting geological and paleontological sites in the area.

For the Kids: Dinosaur Ridge hosts a wide variety of programs for kids, including summer fossil and geology camps, simulated fossil digs, and much more!

Also in the Area: Check out the nearby Morrison Museum, where many excellent Jurassic-age dinosaurs were found.

Contact Info: www.dinoridge.org/

You read that right, you can touch the bones in the Dinosaur Ridge Bone Quarry. And, oh yeah, it was the site of the first-ever *Stegosaurus* discovery.

Touch that dino bone!

What's here?
Dinosaur bones still encased in the rock, and dozens of tracks.

Dinosaur State Park

God bless modern building development! Dinosaur State Park officially opened in 1968, two years after 2,000 dinosaur tracks were accidentally uncovered during the excavation for a new state building. Five hundred tracks are now enclosed within the Exhibit Center's geodesic dome, with the remaining 1,500 remain buried for preservation. (Even dinosaur tracks encased in stone can weather away.) The park allows visitors to make their own plaster casts of dinosaur tracks. This means you can take a dinosaur track home with you!

Dino Sleuthing

Even though some dinosaur footprints—such as these—are very obvious and well preserved, it takes a lot of detective work to figure out what actually made them. And when the trail went cold millions of years ago, the task can be quite daunting indeed. Nevertheless, in this case, there's a good chance the prints were mostly made by *Dilophosaurus* (page 94), a dino made infamous by *Jurassic Park*. You probably remember it as the frilled dinosaur that could spit venom. As it turns out, *Dilophosaurus* didn't have a frill and it probably couldn't spit venom. But it did have a pretty cool crest on its head!

Gift Shop Finds: The park's gift shops features many *Dilophosaurus*-themed items, along with T-shirts, stuffed animals, and fun books.

Location: Rocky Hill, Connecticut.

Type of Site: Museum and enclosed track site.

Age: 200 million years.

Site Rating: ★★★★

Digging: Digging/collecting isn't allowed, but the park allows visitors to make fossil casts from May to October.

For the Kids: The park's Discovery Room features hands-on displays, rocks and minerals, and more!

Also in the Area: It's only a few miles to Hartford, the capital of Connecticut, which is home to much cultural history and a lot of great colonial architecture.

Contact Info: www.dinosaurstatepark.org/

The park allows visitors to make their own plaster casts of dinosaur tracks. How about dinosaur track stepping stones for the garden?!

The park's geodesic dome

What's here?
Dinosaur tracks and plenty of them! Presumably from *Dilophosaurus*.

Dinosaur Valley State Park

George Adams was described as "a very good sculptor." To make a few bucks during the Great Depression he carved dinosaur tracks and sold them to tourists. He found inspiration from real dinosaur tracks at present-day Dinosaur Valley State Park, not far from where he lived. When George's supply of fake tracks ran low, he'd simply make more from the local limestone. Eventually some folks suggested that they saw human footprints alongside the real dinosaur tracks. Next thing ya know good ol' George offered up carved human footprints AND dinosaur tracks in the same rock. Creationists soon latched onto the idea, sparking a one-sided "debate" about humans living alongside dinosaurs.

Humans with Dinosaurs

Everyone agrees on this much: The dinosaur tracks found here are legit. Most of the tracks visible today were left behind by giant sauropod (huge plant-eating) dinosaurs. These tracks were made during the Cretaceous, around 113 million years ago. The real debate, some would say, centers on this question: Were humans walking alongside these dinosaurs? Some would-be "researchers" insist that was the case, pointing to tracks that look vaguely human-like. If this claim were true—it's not!—it would effectively upend all modern science. As it turns out, there's a simple explanation: These so-called human prints are also dinosaur in origin, left by bipedal theropods.

Note: The dinosaur tracks are found along the Paluxy River, so if the water's high, they aren't always visible. Check with the park ahead of time to see if the tracks are visible.

Gift Shop Finds: The park's gift shop offers a variety of track-themed gifts, including pins, refrigerator magnets, T-shirts, and more!

Don't miss the chance to participate in cleaning the dinosaur tracks!

The Paluxy River

What's here?
Dinosaur tracks from sauropods and theropods.

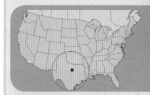

Location: Glen Rose, Texas.

Type of Site: A dinosaur track site.

Age: 113 million years.

Site Rating: ★★★★★

Digging: Digging isn't allowed, but once or twice a year park staff clean the dinosaur tracks, and visitors are allowed to participate. New tracks are uncovered periodically and in need of cleaning. This is fun for the whole family. All equipment is furnished. Wear clothes and shoes suitable for getting wet. Check the website for date and times.

For the Kids: Kids can borrow a Junior Ranger Explorer Pack and receive a pin for completing its activities.

Also in the Area: The site is about an hour from the Waco Mammoth National Monument.

Contact Info:
http://tpwd.texas.gov/state-parks/dinosaur-valley

Ghost Ranch

ABOUT THE SITE

Ghost Ranch may be famous for its connection to the legendary artist Georgia O'Keeffe, but it's even more important in the world of paleontology. *Coelophysis*, one of the earliest known dinosaurs, was found here and eventually became New Mexico's state fossil. Since then many other important fossils have been discovered in the Triassic "red beds" of Ghost Ranch. A popular destination for artists and tourists, Ghost Ranch is also home to two full-fledged museums—the Ruth Hall Museum of Paleontology and the Florence Hawley Ellis Museum of Anthropology. If you're a dino nut (and of course you are!), head to the paleontology museum. It was literally built around a massive block of dinosaur bones giving the museum's prep lab material to study for years to come. The museum also occasionally hosts visits to excavation sites, allowing you to see dino science firsthand.

Dinosaurs and Ghosts at the Ranch

Georgia O'Keeffe knew what she wanted, and it wasn't to be stuck in New York City. When she visited New Mexico for the first time in the 1930s she fell in love with the earth-toned buttes and mesas of this area, ultimately buying a house at Ghost Ranch and a place down the road in Abiquiu. Despite her association with the place, O'Keeffe never owned the ranch proper. But she spent a great deal of time there, and became friends with the various owners. Today, Ghost Ranch offers a number of retreats, a library, and guided tours, including a paleontology tour, a movie tour (the site is a popular filming location), an archaeology tour, and, of course, a Georgia O'Keeffe tour.

If you're interested in getting your hands dirty, the on-site Ruth Hall Museum of Paleontology offers occasional tours of the dig sites and has a volunteer program. In addition, the New Mexico Museum of Natural History and Science in Albuquerque runs volunteer programs for field work here, though only for regular volunteers.

Gift Shop Finds: As far as I know, O'Keeffe never painted any dinosaur bones, but she certainly painted the "red beds" where they are found. A print of one of those works is the perfect keepsake.

Come for the dinosaurs, stay for the modernist art!

At the paleontology museum

What's here?
Coelophysis skeletons piled up in the red sandstones of Ghost Ranch.

Location: Abiquiu, New Mexico.

Type of Site: A museum and sites nearby.

Age: 200 million years.

Site Rating: ★★⭒

Digging: The Ghost Ranch Museum of Paleontology offers occasional tours of the dig sites and has a volunteer program; check out their website.

For the Kids: The site offers activities such as "Dinosaur Bone Dig" and "Plaster Bone Casting."

Also in the Area: The anthropology museum has extensive displays about the many cultures who have lived here, past and present.

Contact Info:
Ghost Ranch:
www.ghostranch.org

New Mexico Museum:
www.nmnaturalhistory.org/

Great Plains Dinosaur Museum

ABOUT THE SITE

If you want to dig for dinosaurs at a real fossil site, sign up—in advance!—with the Great Plains Dinosaur Museum, which operates dinosaur digs from May to August of each year. It's the real thing! They have programs tailored to adults and also some specifically for kids. There's a fee to participate, but you'll be provided with a sack lunch, water, all the necessary tools and equipment, and transportation to and from the site. You'll work beside trained field paleontologists and museum staff who will teach you the techniques. To really immerse yourself in the experience we recommend you book more than one day of digging. Keep in mind this is the real thing and it can get grueling. But unearthing the bones of extinct giants is an unforgettable experience.

Big Sky . . . and Big Dinosaurs

Montana is known as Big Sky country, but that's not the only big thing here. To a dinosaur hunter, Montana means big opportunities: It's home to big digs and big, huge bones. The Great Plains Dinosaur Museum operates seasonal digs in search of dinosaurs. Most of their finds are hadrosaurs (page 104), big duck-billed dinosaurs that fed on plants. So load up the car and head on over to Malta for a true field experience. All fossils discovered are donated to the museum, where they are preserved for future generations.

Gift Shop Finds: The gift shop features a wide variety of dino-themed gifts, from toys and games to educational projects that are well suited for teenagers and adults.

Location: Malta, Montana.

Type of Site: A museum and bone digs.

Age: 76 million years.

Site Rating: ★★★★★

Digging: Great Plains Dinosaur Museum and Field Station is all about helping you dig dinosaurs! They have a variety of programs for kids and adults. See their website for details/pricing.

For the Kids: The museum offers the Junior Paleo Program for 5–10 year olds. It features segments in the lab as well as one in the field at real dinosaur sites.

Also in the Area: Bowdoin National Wildlife Refuge, just northeast of Malta, is famous for bird watching. More than 260 species have been spotted there.

Contact Info: www.greatplainsdinosaurs.org

Great Plains Dinosaur Museum offers the real deal: The chance to participate in a dinosaur dig!

A complete dinosaur skeleton

What's here?
Several types of Cretaceous dinosaurs, including hadrosaurs, ceratopsians, and tyrannosaurs.

Haddonfield Dinosaur Site

Today, Haddonfield, New Jersey, isn't exactly a paleontological hotspot, but it sure was in 1858. That's when a huge, reasonably complete dinosaur skeleton was discovered there. Dinosaurs had been all the rage since their discovery in the 1820s in the United Kingdom, but what had been found up to that point was incomplete. The dinosaur that was discovered in Haddonfield was different. *Hadrosaurus foulkii* was a hadrosaur, one of a group of dinosaurs known as "duck-billed dinosaurs." These large herbivores roamed the Earth during the Cretaceous. The original dinosaur bones (shown above) are now housed in the Academy of Natural Sciences in Philadelphia. But Haddonfield makes the most of its paleontological legacy; there is now a Hadrosaurus Lane as well as a full-size bronze statue of the famous find.

The First Big Find

The year 1858 is an important waypoint in the study of dinosaurs. While traces of dinosaurs such as *Iguanodon* and *Megalosaurus* had been discovered long before in Europe, most of the finds had been fragmentary. That changed when people started finding dinosaurs in North America. In October of that year, a crew led by Philadelphia Academy of Natural Sciences member William Foulke excavated the nearly complete skeleton of a gigantic prehistoric animal from a marl pit on the Haddonfield farm of John Estaugh Hopkins. The bones they found shared similarities with birds and reptiles. On December 14, 1858, at a meeting of the Academy of Natural Sciences, Dr. Joseph Leidy presented a paper describing the anatomy of an almost complete dinosaur, which he named *Hadrosaurus foulkii* in honor of its discoverer, William Foulke. The dinosaur craze had arrived in North America!

Gift Shop Finds: There is no gift shop on-site here, but hadrosaurus.com has a wide variety of items pertaining to "Haddy" the Hadrosaur, including posters, T-shirts, and even commemorative statuettes of the hadrosaur.

Location: Haddonfield, New Jersey.

Type of Site: The original discovery site of the earliest North American dino find.

Age: 73 million years.

Site Rating: ★★

Digging: No digging or collecting.

For the Kids: The site occasionally hosts school groups and runs some educational programs for kids. Kids will love the site's hadrosaur statue, too.

Also in the Area: Haddonfield isn't that far from Philadelphia, which houses the bones of the original hadrosaur find.

Contact Info: www.hadrosaurus.com

After a visit to the discovery site, head on over to Philly to see the real bones of "Haddy" the Hadrosaur!

The fossil discovery site

What's here?
The discovery site of *Hadrosaurus foulkii*, the first dinosaur find in North America.

Nash Dinosaur Track Site

Carlton Nash attended Amherst College amid the throes of the Great Depression. While there, he studied paleontology and enjoyed perusing the school's collection of fossils, most of all the dinosaur footprints from the local region. Carlton soon resolved to find his own fossils, and in 1933 he happened upon a small outcropping of dinosaur tracks. Since he didn't own the land, he kept the find a secret. It took a few years, but in 1939 he finally bought the site. He then went into business quarrying out tracks in the summer and selling them to tourists in the winter. The tradition is now carried on by his son. Tracks are still being found at the site and are available for sale. Thankfully, dinosaur tracks are much more common than dinosaur bones; the many layers of the Nash Site have produced thousands of tracks.

Dinosaur Track Doorstop

Way back in 1802, Pliny Moody was out plowing a field, having a fine day, when out of nowhere, *BAM!* He hits a rock. As if the fact it screwed up his plowshare wasn't bad enough, he now had to get rid of the darned thing! It occurred to him that his home was short a doorstep out front, and that's what the dinosaur track became. Thus we have the first documented evidence of a dinosaur step becoming a human step. Or perhaps we should call it a human stepping-stone where once a dino stepped, in the mud. Or maybe we could say what was once a muddy dino step . . . oh, never mind! Anyway, this discovery would eventually enthrall later generations, as it did Carlton Nash, who was driven to find his own dinosaur tracks, although not for use as doorsteps. He found some and the Nash Dinosaur Track Site was born.

Gift Shop Finds: This is one of the few places you can actually buy a real dinosaur track right from the ground out back. They can be somewhat expensive (especially if they are large or feature many tracks), but the opportunity is unparalleled.

Location: South Hadley, Massachusetts.

Type of Site: A private shop and trackway quarry.

Age: 185 million years.

Site Rating: ★★★

Digging: Sorry, not here!

For the Kids: Just a few miles away in South Hadley, Massachusetts, the Old Firehouse Museum is great for kids.

Also in the Area: Arcadia Wildlife Sanctuary and Mount Tom State Reservation are just up the road in Easthampton, Massachusetts.

Contact Info: www.nashdinosaurtracks.com

This is one gift shop—it sells actual dinosaur tracks—not to miss.

A vintage look at the track site

What's here?
Dinosaur tracks, for sale!

PaleoAdventures

PaleoAdventures is a private venture that works in the badlands of South Dakota, Wyoming and Montana and offers dinosaur dig experiences that are as short as one day. All excavations are on private land. They not only allow the public to participate in digs, but also offer participants the opportunity to take home actual dinosaur fossils, as long as they are not scientifically or commercially significant. If you want to participate, make your reservations well in advance as space is limited and they fill up fast.

First, Dinosaurs, then Sturgis?

Like motorcycles? Well, lucky for you, PaleoAdventures is only a few miles north of Sturgis, home to the nation's most popular motorcycle rally. Get off your chopper and dig in! You can spend as little as one day here or stay as long as a few weeks.

Amateur and commercial fossil digging is one of the hot debate topics in contemporary paleontology. Vertebrate fossils are generally rare, and dinosaur fossils are even rarer. That's why fossil hunting for vertebrates on public lands is strictly regulated, as it should be. But private land is another story. Collecting on private land is entirely legal, though some academics question if it is ethical. Proponents argue that there are not enough paleontologists to excavate all of the fossils that are out there—which is true—and if fossils are just left to sit, they'll gradually erode and be lost to science—which is also true. Both of these claims are essentially indisputable. The real test, by our standards, is where the fossils end up. Reputable companies like PaleoAdventures see to it that the important finds go to museums, where they can be studied by researchers in perpetuity.

Gift Shop Finds: PaleoAdventures offers some of its finds for sale, as long as they are not scientifically significant.

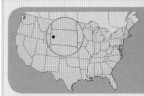

Location: Belle Fourche, South Dakota.

Type of Site: Summer dig programs.

Age: 75 million years.

Site Rating: ★★★★★

Digging: PaleoAdventures works in South Dakota, Wyoming and Montana and offers up dig experiences as short as one day. But call ahead to see what options there are for your time period.

For the Kids: Special programs for kids are offered at schools throughout the region.

Also in the Area: Sturgis, South Dakota, the site of the famous motorcycle festival, is just a few miles north.

Contact Info: www.paleoadventures.com/index.html

PaleoAdventures offers dinosaur digs and the opportunity to keep some real dinosaur bones!

A fine find

What's here?
Hadrosaurs, ceratopsians and tyrannosaurids.

Petrified Forest National Park

Many years ago Paul Bunyan and Babe the Blue Ox stopped here for some recreational tree cutting before traveling to the Great North Woods. They enjoyed the scenery and the variety of animals that lived in the region, including dinosaurs. The dinos found here were fairly small, like the bipedal *Coelophysis*, but don't let that hold you back. The park is, of course, most famous for its giant trees turned to stone. But there's a catch: The giant trees found here didn't grow here; they grew elsewhere and were transported here. Massive floods uprooted the trees and washed them downstream to this area whereupon they were quickly buried. Paul Bunyan and Babe stood on the banks and watched the whole thing in amazement.

Agate Logs and Early Dinosaurs

Petrified Forest National Park is not just about petrified forests. Oh, it's got plenty of that, alright, but there's tons more to it than you'd think by the title. Get tuned in at the Painted Desert Visitor Center and the Rainbow Forest Museum. They're great places to get your bearings, see some great displays—including mounted fossil skeletons—and learn about the park.

If it's pretty fossilized wood you're after, head to the southern portion of the park, where you can see the incredible Jasper Forest and the Agate House, which is over a thousand years old. The northern part of the park is most famous for the amazing Painted Desert, which lives up to its name quite admirably.

Taking a leisurely drive is one great way to enjoy the park, as it's easy to access the very scenic overlooks. You can always stop and look around or take a hike on—or off—one of the maintained trails. If you're feeling more adventurous, the park also offers a number of backcountry hiking options.

Gift Shop Finds: There are two gift shops on-site, and if you want petrified wood, you can purchase some there. It is responsibly sourced from legal sources. Collecting is *not* allowed at the park.

From the massive petrified logs and the agate house to the petroglyphs on-site, there are dozens of reasons to visit.

One of the park's earliest residents

What's here?
Incredible petrified wood logs, petroglyphs, and early dinosaurs.

Location: Holbrook, Arizona.

Type of Site: Several museums (and trails) featuring bones and petrified wood.

Age: 225 million years.

Site Rating: ★★★★★

Digging: No digging or collecting. But there is plenty of petrified wood from private lands for sale at the shops in Holbrook.

For the Kids: Kids can participate in the Junior Ranger program.

Also in the Area: Meteor Crater is just to the west and a must-see. Even farther west is Sunset Crater; its crater is the remnant of an extinct volcano.

Contact Info:
www.nps.gov/pefo/index.htm

Purgatoire River Dinosaur Track Site

It might be named Purgatoire, but it's actually not that bad. You know those glossy magazine articles you occasionally see about dinosaurs and how much we can learn about them from their preserved footprints? Well, many of the pictures from those articles are from this site, located in the Picketwire Wilderness. This is one of the largest dinosaur track sites in the country. Even better, many of the impressions show good detail. If you sign up for a guided auto tour, which is led by the U.S. Forest Service, you get to drive up quite close to the tracks. If you opt to hike there yourself it's a bit of a trek, albeit a scenic one.

Predator and Prey

Many of these tracks are thought to be contemporary with one another, having been stomped into the soft mud about the same time. There's even speculation—based on the trackways in evidence here—that some crafty carnivores were in hot pursuit of an Extra Value Meal. That is, one of the tasty sauropods that was cruising its away across the mudflats. Of course, we don't know the end of the story or even if they went hungry that night, but it's amazing to think that you're walking where huge predators like the *Allosaurus* may have once hunted monster prey.

Gift Shop Finds: There is no gift shop on-site, nor any other buildings, for that matter. But there are lots of tracks spread over a quarter mile, so there's plenty to see!

To put it simply, this site boasts some of the finest dinosaur tracks on the planet.

This place has tons of tracks!

What's here?
Apatosaurus and *Allosaurus* tracks.

Location: La Junta, Colorado.

Type of Site: World-famous dinosaur tracks.

Age: 150 million years.

Site Rating: ★★★★★

Digging: The Denver Museum of Nature and Science offers ongoing volunteer opportunities throughout the region, some of which take place in the Picketwire Wilderness, where these tracks are located. Contact them at www.dmns.org for more info.

For the Kids: The Denver Museum of Nature and Science is great to visit with kids.

Also in the Area: If you hike to this site, you'll pass the remains of an old ghost town and cemetery along the way.

Contact Info: www.recreation.gov/ tourParkDetail.do? contractCode=NRSO& parkId=74974

Red Fleet State Park

ABOUT THE SITE

Around 200 million years ago, dinosaurs inhabited the land in and around present-day Vernal, which is now home to Red Fleet State Park and one of the gateways to Dinosaur National Monument. The park boasts one of the better dinosaur track sites in the region, with hundreds of clear dinosaur tracks visible in the park's red sandstone beds. A popular hiking and camping destination, it is also home to Red Fleet Reservoir, which is known affectionately as "Little Lake Powell" and is popular with anglers, boaters and swimmers.

Racing Dinosaurs

To reach the dinosaur tracks at this park, you need to take a hike. So do it! The 1.5-mile trail to the tracks is a little strenuous, as it includes several uphill and downhill sections. The best viewing times are early morning or late afternoon, as the tracks are somewhat difficult to see when the sun is directly overhead. Also, keep in mind that in spring and early summer when the water levels are higher, the tracks are often submerged by Red Fleet Reservoir. Here's a quiz: How long do you think it would take the dinosaurs to make the 1.5 mile hike to the site? Hint: They are attributed to *Dilophosaurus*, which could run 30 mph. (Answer: three minutes.)

Gift Shop Finds: There's no gift shop on-site, but there are plenty of dinosaur-related items in Vernal, which really plays up its dinosaur ties. The town even features a large *Tyrannosaurus rex* statue that is dressed seasonally.

Location: Vernal, Utah.

Type of Site: Dinosaur track site next to a reservoir.

Age: 200 million years.

Site Rating: ★★★

Digging: No digging or collecting. Self-guided and sometimes ranger-led interpretive hikes to track site.

For the Kids: There isn't that much in the park but the Utah Field House in Vernal has special programs for kids.

Also in the Area: The Utah Field House of Natural History is well worth visiting. And, don't forget the fabulous Dinosaur National Monument!

Contact Info:
Red Fleet State Park:
http://stateparks.utah.gov/parks/red-fleet/discover/

Utah Field House:
http://stateparks.utah.gov/parks/utah-field-house/

Enjoy seeing the dinosaur tracks at Red Fleet State Park, then head to Vernal for some dinosaur Americana: roadside dinosaur sculptures!

One of Vernal's dinosaur statues

What's here?
Lots of tracks of bipedal dinosaurs, some of which are attributed to *Dilophosaurus*.

Red Gulch Dinosaur Track Site

ABOUT THE SITE

At the Bureau of Land Management's Red Gulch Dinosaur Track Site, it's easy to imagine yourself as a dinosaur stomping around the wilderness. Picture it: It's 167 million years ago, and you're walking along an ocean shoreline with dozens of other dinosaurs, looking to pick up a bite of lunch from what washed up on the last high tide. The ground is soft and your feet sink down in the thick ooze, leaving a clear footprint with every step you take. But the pickings are slim, so you and your pals wander off in search of a Wendy's instead . . .

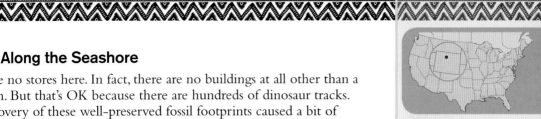

A Walk Along the Seashore

There are no stores here. In fact, there are no buildings at all other than a bathroom. But that's OK because there are hundreds of dinosaur tracks. The discovery of these well-preserved fossil footprints caused a bit of a stir in the paleo world and has altered our current views about the paleoenvironment of the middle Jurassic in the region. Specifically, this area was once periodically inundated by a sea, so it was thought that no dinosaur tracks would be found here. But here there are, so scientists have had to revise their assumptions about the area. While the exact species isn't clear, the tracks appear to have been made by theropods, a group of bipedal dinosaurs that ate meat.

The track site is located off the Red Gulch/Alkali National Backcountry Byway, not far from Shell, Wyoming. Check out the BLM's website for details and directions. There is a boardwalk that heads to the track site.

Gift Shop Finds: There's no gift shop on-site, but Thermopolis has all sorts of souvenir shops.

Location: Worland, Wyoming.

Type of Site: A dinosaur track site.

Age: 167 million years.

Site Rating: ★★★

Digging: Sorry, not here!

For the Kids: School groups and kids' programs can be set up by special arrangement.

Also in the Area: Thirty minutes southwest is Thermopolis, site of the famous hot springs and home to the Wyoming Dinosaur Center. The Big Horn Mountains are thirty minutes to the northwest.

Contact Info: www.blm.gov/wy/st/en/field_offices/Worland/Tracksite.html

Head to Red Gulch to see these tracks, which weren't even supposed to exist!

The main body of tracks

What's here?
Theropod dinosaur tracks.

St. George Dinosaur Discovery Site at Johnson Farm

This is one of the finest dinosaur track sites in the world. Tracks from a variety of different dinosaurs have been found here and examples include *Dilophosaurus* (depicted as the dinosaur that could "spit venom" in the movie *Jurassic Park*), *Megapnosaurus*, a primitive theropod, and *Scutellosaurus*, a relatively small armored dinosaur that probably walked on two legs. Deposited around 185 million years ago, the level of detail found in the tracks is astounding: There are even places where skin impressions have been cast in fine relief.

The Doctor and His Dinosaurs

It could be said Dr. Sheldon Johnson had a good eye for unusual things. But, then again, that was his job: He was an optometrist. In 2000, he started clearing land on his property in order to construct a building, but he stopped when he noticed what appeared to be tracks. Some looked like impressions in the rock, but others occurred in high relief, and stuck out of the rock. Being a scientist Dr. Johnson had the presence of mind to call in the experts. He soon discovered his land was a veritable treasure trove of dinosaur footprints—some of the finest ever found!—nearly 200 million years in the making. Not long thereafter Sheldon and his wife LaVerna set up a foundation dedicated to preserving the site and helped garner funds to build a museum. Today the Dinosaur Discovery Site at Johnson Farm is a thriving testimony to doing the right dinosaurian thing.

Gift Shop Finds: The gift shop offers a variety of high-quality resin casts of the tracks found on-site, and these make a great keepsake after a visit.

Location: St. George, Utah.

Type of Site: A small museum with an enclosed track site.

Age: 185 million years.

Site Rating: ★★★★⯨

Digging: St. George Dinosaur Discovery Site welcomes volunteers from the area who can commit to scheduled hours. Opportunities include digging, fossil preparation, curation of specimens and guiding tours.

For the Kids: The site hosts periodic special programs for kids. An event known as Dino Days in Dixie honors the discovery of the site and is held each May.

Also in the Area: Not far from St. George, Zion National Park is one of the great natural wonders of North America.

Contact Info: www.dinosite.org/

Kids will love the museum's dino park, which features a sandbox where kids can make dinosaur tracks with replica dino feet.

One of the site's tracks

What's here?
Tracks from *Dilophosaurus*, *Megapnosaurus* and *Scutellosaurus*, among others.

Tuba City Dinosaur Track Site

You simply won't find better "dinosaurian paleoichnofauna" (dinosaur tracks) with this kind of easy access. They are literally right next to the parking area! The variety of tracks and the excellent state of their preservation make this one of the best public sites of its kind in the Southwest. The dinosaurs in question lived during the Jurassic Period some 193 million years ago. The tracks were deposited on mudflats that eventually hardened into the rock that you see here. The tracks were left by theropods—carnivorous dinosaurs that walked on two legs. The site is on the Navajo Reservation so you're required to have a guide, though there is not a set fee; it's by donation only. But be sure to give up at least a few bucks to help the local economy.

Dino Tracks and Ancient Petroglyphs

After you are done touring the track site, be sure to ask the guides about the incredible petroglyphs in nearby Moenave, a small settlement just to the north of the dino tracks. If you're lucky, they'll take you to them and you'll be able to witness one of the finest petroglyph sites in the state. It's only a five-minute car ride from the dinosaur tracks, but you must hire a guide to visit. The spot is important to local tribes, and they may not grant you access on certain days. If you're allowed to visit, consider yourself lucky and be sure to tip your guide an extra-generous amount. If they don't take you, tough luck: you can't go there unescorted.

Gift Shop Finds: Most of the time there are gift stands set up by the local tribe at the track site parking area where they sell goods made by local Navajo.

Easily accessible dinosaur tracks and perhaps a look at petroglyphs, what could be better?

Some the incredible petroglyphs nearby

Location: Tuba City, Arizona.

Type of Site: Track site with guides from the area Navajo tribe.

Age: 193 million years.

Site Rating: ★★★★

Digging: No digging or collecting. Navajo guides offer interpretive hikes around trackways.

For the Kids: In Tuba City kids will love the Navajo Interactive Museum.

Also in the Area: This site is located close to so many great natural wonders, it'll take you a month to see half of them. Examples include: Sunset Crater, the Grand Canyon, Monument Valley, Elgin Pueblo, Walnut Canyon, and Wapatki.

Contact Info:
www.experiencehopi.com/dinosaur-tracks.html

What's here?
Theropod dinosaur tracks and a chance to see some incredible petroglyphs.

Two Medicine Dinosaur Center

ABOUT THE SITE

The Two Medicine Dinosaur Center can feel a little crowded at times, but that's understand-able as it's likely the only place you'll ever see a fully mounted *Seismosaurus* model. A giant among giants, *Seismosaurus* was an incredible 137 feet long! The museum also features a dinosaur bone that you're allowed to touch! Two Medicine Dinosaur Center offers another bonus: For a fee, you can tag along on one of the museum's dinosaur digs (they offer a number of flexible scheduling options) and there's no doubt you'll find dinosaur bones.

Joining a Real Dig

Let's face it, there's not much money in being a paleontologist. Most of the time it's a starving-artist lifestyle and the shoestring income can get difficult to justify when you get to the point of settling down and raising a family. That's where this site comes in; the Two Medicine Dinosaur Center's dig programs allow you to participate in a real dinosaur dig, and they offer an incredible amount of flexibility. If you have only half a day or day to burn, you still can get out and dig dinos for real!

Gift Shop Finds: The Dinosaur Center's museum sells casts of dinosaur and other fossils, enabling you to take home a *Tyrannosaurus rex* tooth, a *Megalodon* tooth, and more.

Location: Bynum, Montana.

Type of Site: A museum with bone digs.

Age: 100–75 million years.

Site Rating: ★★★★★

Digging: You can pay to participate in short- or long-term digs alongside a team of professional staff paleontologists.

For the Kids: Loads of programs for kids and young adults; the museum also features a dinosaur bone that you can actually touch!

Also in the Area: While you are in this part of Montana, you're not very far from Glacier National Park, one of the gems of the National Park Service.

Contact Info: www.tmdinosaurcenter.org

The *Seismosaurus* model is pretty staggering, and you can touch a dinosaur bone here, too!

You can buy a cast replica of a *T. rex* skull

What's here?
Fossils of hadrosaurs, ceratopsians, and tyrannosaurs, along with a huge *Seismosaurus* model.

Wyoming Dinosaur Center

Thermopolis is hugely famous for its claim as the home of the largest hot spring in the world. But if you ask me, it's home to something even better: The Wyoming Dinosaur Center. Replete with both dinosaur and non-dino fossils alike, the center features two *Velociraptors*, marine reptiles (think sea monsters!), and even a mounted skeleton of a *Tyrannosaurus rex* attacking a *Triceratops*. Better yet, for a fee, you can participate in an actual dig at a dinosaur site. This is a world-class paleontological destination that you, as a dinosaur connoisseur, cannot miss!

More Than Just Hot Springs

You've packed up the family and you're finally on the road. You've set your sights on Yellowstone and are driving like hell to get there before the kids go bonkers (a hopeless cause). If you're headed to Yellowstone and entering through one of the East Entrances, you will not want to miss this gold mine of dinosauria. One of the greatest collection of dino bones and sites in the world is located in the rolling hills at the base of the Wind River Mountain Range. This place is home to the only real *Archaeopteryx* on display in North America. *Archaeopteryx* was one of the earliest birds, and it is one of the most important fossils ever found. The museum also features tours to a real dig site, where visitors can see where fearsome *Allosaurus* fed on huge sauropods—there are even bones with tooth marks on them to prove it!

Gift Shop Finds: The gift shop boasts everything from rocks and fossils to *Dino-Opoly,* a perfect board game for your resident dinosaur nut.

The site features a real *Archaeopteryx*, a bone bed that has produced *Allosaurus* skeletons, and even a giant model of a *Tyrannosaurus rex* doing battle with a *Triceratops*.

Just one of the fine fossils on display

What's here?
Camarasaurus, *Diplodocus*, and *Apatosaurus* fossils.

Location: Thermopolis, Wyoming.

Type of Site: A museum and bone digs.

Age: 175 million years

Site Rating: ★★★★★

Digging: The Shovel Ready Dig Program takes your visit to the next level! You can walk in, sign up and dig all in the same day. Reservations are first-come, first-served. Space is limited, so be sure to grab a spot. Participants are provided with every-thing they need to assist in a dig.

For the Kids: The site hosts special dig programs for kids and a Dinosaur Academy for high school students.

Also in the Area: Thermo-polis is the gateway to both Grand Teton and Yellow-stone National Parks.

Contact Info: www.wyodino.org

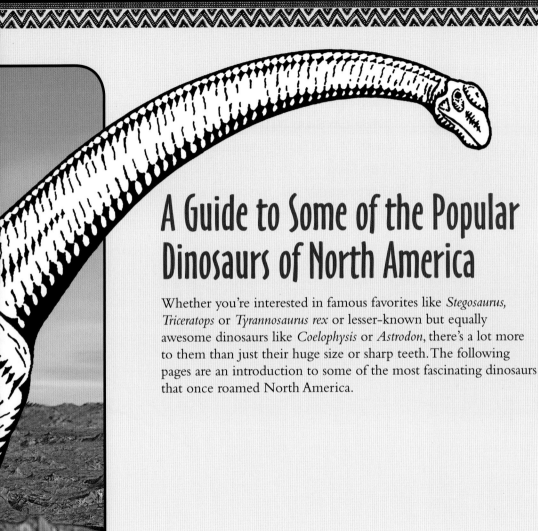

A Guide to Some of the Popular Dinosaurs of North America

Whether you're interested in famous favorites like *Stegosaurus,
Triceratops* or *Tyrannosaurus rex* or lesser-known but equally
awesome dinosaurs like *Coelophysis* or *Astrodon*, there's a lot more
to them than just their huge size or sharp teeth. The following
pages are an introduction to some of the most fascinating dinosaurs
that once roamed North America.

Albertosaurus

(Al-bear-toh-soar-us)

Dinosaur Group: Tyrannosaur

Meaning of Name: "Alberta lizard"

Maximum Size: 30 feet long

Lived: 71–68 million years ago (Cretaceous Period)

Diet: Meat

Discovered: 1884, by Joseph Tyrrell; named by Henry Fairfield Osborn in 1905

Locations in North America: MT, NM, WY, Alberta

Albertosaurus are famous for their teeth, and for good reason. An adult generally had 58 teeth in its large mouth and that made this bad boy the top dog of its neighborhood. Scientists have found sites with dozens of *Albertosaurus* individuals grouped together, and this suggests herding or, at the least, coordinated pack behavior. Now *that's* a terrifying proposition.

 Fun Facts:

Like *Tyrannosaurus rex*, *Albertosaurus* had a large head and a mouth brimming with more than four dozen long, sharp teeth.

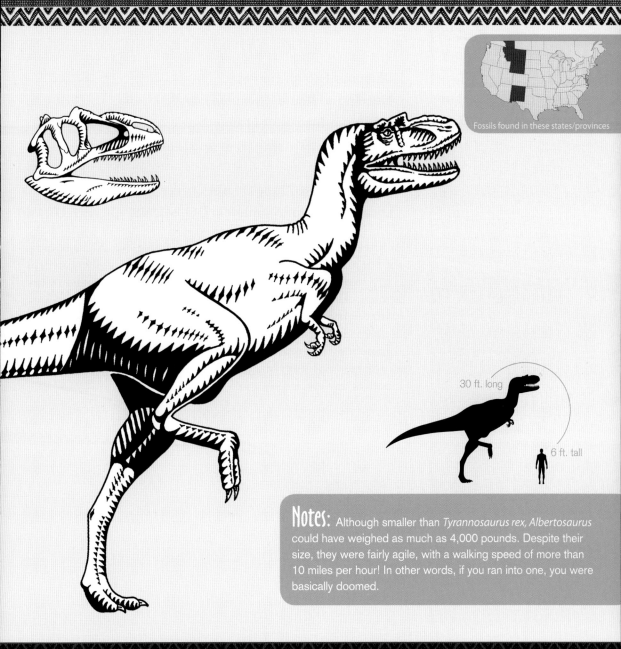

Fossils found in these states/provinces

30 ft. long

6 ft. tall

Notes: Although smaller than *Tyrannosaurus rex*, *Albertosaurus* could have weighed as much as 4,000 pounds. Despite their size, they were fairly agile, with a walking speed of more than 10 miles per hour! In other words, if you ran into one, you were basically doomed.

Allosaurus

(Al-oh-soar-us)

Dinosaur Group: Carnosaur

Meaning of Name: "Different lizard"

Maximum Size: 40 feet long

Lived: 155–150 million years ago (Jurassic Period)

Diet: Meat

Discovered: 1877, by Othniel Charles Marsh

Locations in North America: CO, MT, NM, OK, SD, UT, WY

At first glance, *Allosaurus* might look something like a *Tyrannosaurus rex*, but looks can be deceiving, as they aren't that closely related. In fact, *Allosaurus* came onto the dinosaur scene a full 78 million years before its larger cousin made an appearance. An adult *Allosaurus* may have weighed more than two tons (4,000 pounds), and perhaps even double that. Like most other dinosaurs, *Allosaurus* shed its teeth continuously and replaced them with new ones. It had an average of 64 knife-sharp teeth in its mouth at any given time.

 Fun Facts:

Allosaurus was at the top of the food chain during its reign in the Jurassic.

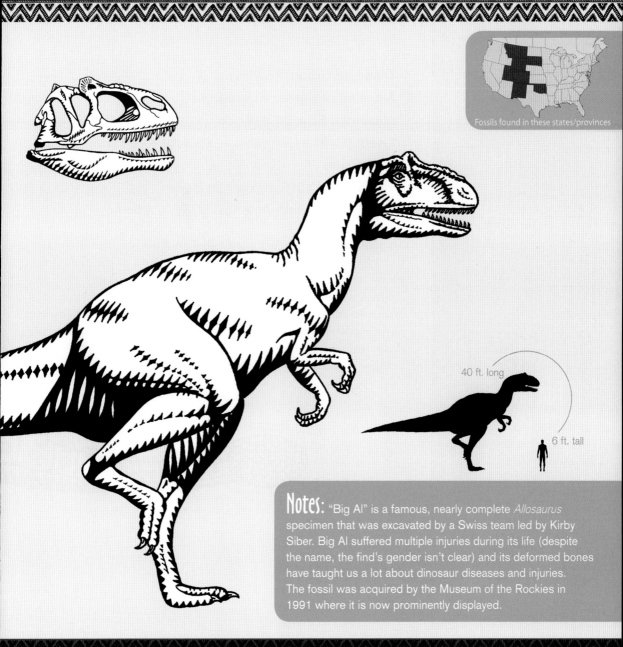

Fossils found in these states/provinces

40 ft. long

6 ft. tall

Notes: "Big Al" is a famous, nearly complete *Allosaurus* specimen that was excavated by a Swiss team led by Kirby Siber. Big Al suffered multiple injuries during its life (despite the name, the find's gender isn't clear) and its deformed bones have taught us a lot about dinosaur diseases and injuries. The fossil was acquired by the Museum of the Rockies in 1991 where it is now prominently displayed.

Ankylosaurus
(Ann-kye-loh-soar-us)

Dinosaur Group: Ankylosaur

Meaning of Name: "Fused lizard"

Maximum Size: 21 feet long

Lived: 68–66 million years ago (Cretaceous Period)

Diet: Plants

Discovered: 1908, by Barnum Brown

Locations in North America: MT, WY, Alberta

Sometimes called the "armored tanks" of dinosaurs, *Ankylosaurus* had a large, stocky body that was really armored, so the nickname is pretty accurate. *Ankylosaurus* is most notable for its skin, which was covered with hard, bony "osteoderms" that served as a sort of plate armor. In addition, it had a club-like tail that it could use to dissuade any would-be predators. Ankylosaurs were also notable because their skulls had extensive nasal passages, suggesting that perhaps they could vocalize and communicate with one another.

 Fun Facts:

Ankylosaurus had a big knobby mass on the end of its tail that it could swing around and use as a highly lethal club to protect itself.

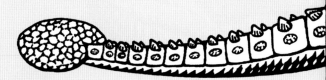

Fossils found in these states/provinces

21 ft. long

6 ft. tall

Apatosaurus

(A-pat-oh-soar-us)

Dinosaur Group: Diplodocid

Meaning of Name: "Deceptive lizard"

Maximum Size: 75 feet long

Lived: 152–150 million years ago (Jurassic Period)

Diet: Plants

Discovered: 1877, by Othniel Charles Marsh

Locations in North America: AZ, CO, NM, OK, SD, UT, WY

First described in 1877, this sauropod was one of the big guys. For a long time scientists thought that *Brontosaurus* and *Apatosaurus* were the same species, but new research concludes that they were separate (though related) groups. *Apatosaurus's* long neck had unusual air sacs that made it lighter, longer, and more flexible; it also had very long ribs, giving it a huge chest size. When ordering T-shirts it definitely had to buy size 10,000XL.

 Fun Facts:

The tail of *Apatosaurus* was so long and light that researchers now think that it was probably used as a whip for communication with other members of its species and maybe even used to scare off predators.

Notes: Up until the mid-twentieth century, it was generally thought that *Apatosaurus* and its other large sauropod relatives were too massive to carry their own weight. Artist recreations from back in the day showed these dinos dragging their sorry butts around in swamps and marshes. Today we know that they could get around just fine and kept their bodies upright off the ground.

Fossils found in these states/provinces

75 ft. long

6 ft. tall

Astrodon

(Astro-don)

Dinosaur Group: Brachiosaurid

Meaning of Name: "Star tooth"

Maximum Size: 60 feet long

Lived: 112 million years ago (Cretaceous Period)

Diet: Plants

Discovered: 1858, by Philip Tyson; first scientifically described by Joseph Leidy in 1865

Locations in North America: MD, OK, TX

Maryland isn't exactly known as a dinosaur hotspot, but that doesn't mean dinos didn't live here; for proof, consider *Astrodon*. Now known as the Maryland state dinosaur, it was first scientifically described by Joseph Leidy in 1865, the year the Civil War ended. It got its far-out-sounding name not as reference to space aliens but based on the unusual star-like shape of its teeth. While *Astrodon* fossils are incomplete, researchers think it probably resembled a small *Brachiosaurus*.

 Fun Facts:

The state dinosaur of Maryland, *Astrodon* is only known from fossil fragments, as no complete skeletons of it have ever been found.

Fossils found in these states/provinces

60 ft. long

6 ft. tall

Notes: The first *Astrodon* teeth were discovered in 1858 amid the clays of an old iron pit. For whatever reason, the discovery site was known as "Swampoodle" and the location of the site was once thought to be lost. Thanks to a good deal of detective work by paleontologist Peter Kranz, the site has been rediscovered. Wouldn't you know it, it's not far from another dino fossil-bearing area, which is known, appropriately enough, as Dinosaur Park in Laurel, Maryland (to visit, see page 32).

Camarasaurus

(Ka-mare-uh-soar-us)

Dinosaur Group: Camarasaurid

Meaning of Name: "Chambered lizard"

Maximum Size: 75 feet long

Lived: 150–112 million years ago (Jurassic Period)

Diet: Plants

Discovered: 1877, by Oramel W. Lucas; scientifically described by Edward Drinker Cope

Locations in North America: CO, MT, NM, UT, WY

When *Camarasaurus* bones were first found in 1877, the discoverer, Oramel Lucas, brought them to town in a less-than-ceremonious fashion: on five wagons, where they were promptly put on display and then shipped to Edward Drinker Cope, one of the most famous paleontologists of his day. At the time it was thought *Camarasaurus* had a typical medium-length neck, but 50 years later a more-complete skeleton was found, and scientists realized that *Camarasaurus's* neck was three times longer than originally thought!

 Fun Facts:

Camarasaurus had very stout teeth that were replaced every two months!

Because they've found sites with multiple animals preserved next to each other, some paleontologists believe that *Camarasaurus* traveled in family groups, much as elephants do today.

Fossils found in these states/provinces

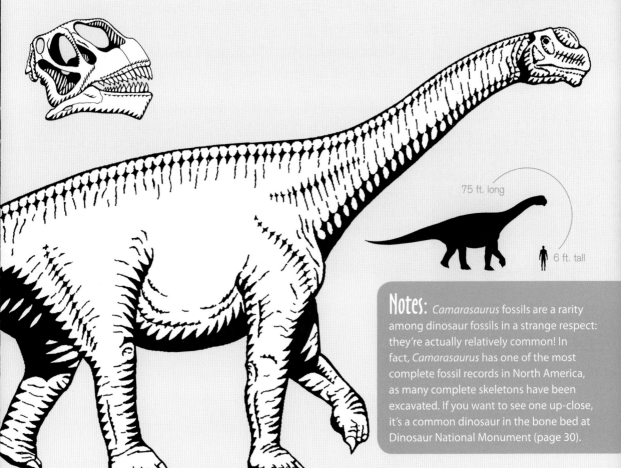

75 ft. long

6 ft. tall

Notes: *Camarasaurus* fossils are a rarity among dinosaur fossils in a strange respect: they're actually relatively common! In fact, *Camarasaurus* has one of the most complete fossil records in North America, as many complete skeletons have been excavated. If you want to see one up-close, it's a common dinosaur in the bone bed at Dinosaur National Monument (page 30).

Centrosaurus

(Sen-troh-soar-us)

Dinosaur Group: Ceratopsid
Meaning of Name: "Pointed lizard"
Maximum Size: 30 feet long
Lived: 84–70 million years ago (Cretaceous Period)
Diet: Plants
Discovered: 1905, by Lawrence Lambe
Locations in North America: MT, Alberta

Centrosaurus had a particularly cool-looking frill, not to mention a massive central horn on its nose, all of which gave it the appearance of some kind of giant gnarly rhino. Despite its looks, the frill wasn't very thick or solid, so it appears that *Centrosaurus* used its frill more for display than defense, just as some lizards do today. Near Hilda, Alberta, fourteen individual *Centrosaurus* bone beds have been discovered, and they are positively littered with bones, leading researchers to speculate that *Centrosaurus* may have traveled in large herds.

Fun Facts:

With a name that means "pointed lizard" you might think that *Centrosaurus* gets its name from its large nasal horn. But it doesn't; instead, the name refers to the strange pair of frill horns that hook forward over the top of its skull.

Fossils found in these states/provinces

30 ft. long

6 ft. tall

Ceratosaurus

(Seh-rat-oh-soar-us)

Dinosaur Group: Ceratosaur

Meaning of Name: "Horned lizard"

Maximum Size: 20 feet long

Lived: 155–150 million years ago (Jurassic Period)

Diet: Meat

Discovered: 1884, by Othniel Charles Marsh

Locations in North America: CO, UT

Ceratosaurus was similar in appearance to *Allosaurus* but had a bigger head in respect to its body size. One would think that an animal with a name like "horned lizard" would be pretty fearsome-looking, but its "horn" was really no big deal, certainly nothing like the horns of *Triceratops* or *Styracosaurus*. It's more like a "hornlet" than anything rhino-like. Scientists speculate that the horn was more for display than defense. But, lest you think *Ceratosaurus* was a wimp, if you saw it and its razor-sharp teeth, you'd definitely want to run the other way.

Fun Facts:

With a row of hard, bony protrusions sticking out of its back, *Ceratosaurus* is one of the only theropods known to have armor.

Notes: *Ceratosaurus* had a peculiarly deep and flexible tail, which was comparable to that of a crocodile. Bob Bakker suggested this may indicate that *Ceratosaurus* was an excellent swimmer, allowing it to hunt for fish and other aquatic fauna.

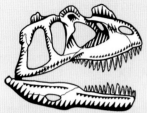

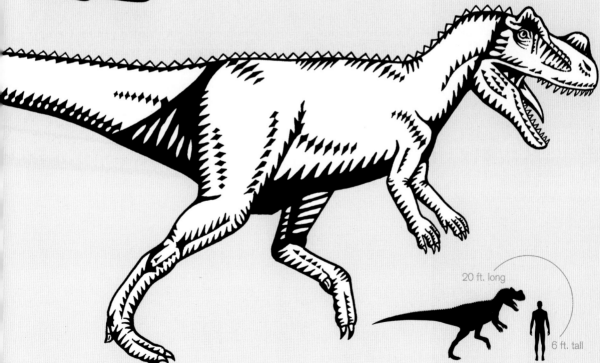

20 ft. long

6 ft. tall

Coelophysis

(Seal-oh-fye-sus)

Dinosaur Group: Coelophysid
Meaning of Name: "Hollow form"
Maximum Size: 10 feet long
Lived: 221–189 million years ago (Triassic Period)
Diet: Meat
Discovered: 1889, by Edward Drinker Cope
Locations in North America: AZ, NM, TX

Coelophysis was an early bipedal dinosaur that lived in the Southwest and was an inhabitant of Ghost Ranch, the New Mexico hamlet that is more famous as a former home of the acclaimed painter Georgia O'Keeffe. While at the ranch, she undoubtedly walked right over many dinosaur skeletons, but never knew it. She was, however, obsessed by bones, so when dinosaurs were discovered at Ghost Ranch, she became interested in the bone quarry, and obtained permission to visit. Sadly, she never put dinosaur bones in her art.

 **Fun Facts:**

Small and fast, this early predatory dinosaur is now the state dinosaur of New Mexico.

Fossils found in these states/provinces

10 ft. long

6 ft. tall

Notes: At Ghost Ranch, literally thousands of skeletons of *Coelophysis* have been uncovered. Such mass graves suggest that *Coelophysis* may have been a herding animal.

Corythosaurus

(Core-rith-oh-soar-us)

Dinosaur Group: Hadrosaur

Meaning of Name: "Helmet lizard"

Maximum Size: 33 feet long

Lived: 77–75 million years ago (Cretaceous Period)

Diet: Plants

Discovered: 1914, by Barnum Brown

Locations in North America: MT, Alberta

With a name meaning "Helmet Lizard" you'd think its headgear might be a tad more impressive. Instead, while the "helmet" that *Corythosaurus* had may have protected its noggin a little, it doesn't have anything on the super helmet of *Pachycephalosaurus* (page 112). In the case of *Corythosaurus* the "helmet" was full of nasal cavities, so it was likely used more for display and communication than as a defensive measure.

Fun Facts:

Most of the *Corythosaurus* discoveries indicate that this dinosaur probably lived in wooded areas.

Fossils found in these states/provinces

33 ft. long

6 ft. tall

Daspletosaurus

(Dass-pleat-oh-soar-us)

Dinosaur Group: Tyrannosaur

Meaning of Name: "Frightful lizard"

Maximum Size: 30 feet long

Lived: 77–74 million years ago (Cretaceous Period)

Diet: Meat

Discovered: 1921, by Charles Sternberg; scientifically described by Dale Russell in 1970

Locations in North America: MT, WY, Alberta

Daspletosaurus looked like a *Tyrannosaurus*, acted like one, and probably smelled like one, but it wasn't *Tyrannosaurus*. Size is the primary difference between them; *Daspletosaurus* was a bit smaller than *Tyrannosaurus rex*. However, like *T. rex,* it had a huge skull—over three feet long!—with a mouth full of long steak-knife teeth that it knew how to use.

 Fun Facts:

Much of *Daspletosaurus's* skull bones were fused together for added strength and chopping power. Some skulls show non-lethal bite marks, suggesting that perhaps these dinosaurs sparred with each other.

Fossils found in these states/provinces

30 ft. long

6 ft. tall

Deinonychus
(Die-non-ick-cuss)

Dinosaur Group: Dromaeosaur

Meaning of Name: "Terrible claw"

Maximum Size: 11 feet long

Lived: 112–109 million years ago (Cretaceous Period)

Diet: Meat

Discovered: 1931, by Barnum Brown; scientifically described by John Ostrom in 1969

Locations in North America: MD, MT, OK, WY

You don't want to get caught in a dark alley with *Deinonychus*. He—or she—might be relatively short, but with its lethal sickle-claw it could easily slice and dice your mammalian haunches and eat you for lunch!

Despite their fearsome claw it's not clear if *Deinonychus* were predators or scavengers, and they may well have been both. *Deinonychus* teeth have been found in association with some large dinosaur bones, but this doesn't necessarily mean that a *Deinonychus* was responsible for the kill, as it could simply have been scavenging.

Fun Facts:

The original North American raptor, this guy was small and agile and may have hunted in packs.

It has been speculated that *Deinonychus* may have had feathers like other small, bipedal Cretaceous dinosaurs. If they did, their bone structure indicates they were probably not adapted for flight, instead perhaps being used for thermoregulation, courtship or some other purpose.

Fossils found in these states/provinces

11 ft. long

6 ft. tall

Dilophosaurus

(Die-loaf-oh-soar-us)

Dinosaur Group: Dilophosaur

Meaning of Name: "Two-crested lizard"

Maximum Size: 23 feet long

Lived: 195–189 million years ago (Jurassic Period)

Diet: Meat

Discovered: 1942, by Jesse Williams;
scientifically described by Samuel Welles in 1970

Locations in North America: AZ

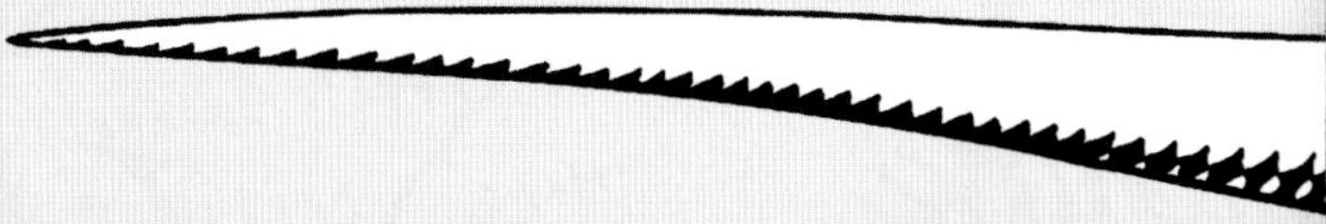

Fun Facts:

With its distinctive double-crest, *Dilophosaurus* was one of the earliest dinosaurs known to have serious ornamentation on its skull.

This is a dinosaur with some headgear. *Dilophosaurus* is famous for its distinctive double crest, but it's not exactly clear what its function was, making this dino a hotly debated topic since its discovery. Even though it looked cool, the crests were pretty fragile, so they were probably used as a display feature more than for aggression or defense. *Dilophosaurus* was a quick, bipedal predator and one of the largest theropods in its environment. Its upper jaw was especially gnarly looking—there was a prominent gap between the front row of teeth and those behind it—lending it a sinister, almost crocodillian look.

23 ft. long

6 ft. tall

Notes: *Dilophosaurus* is one rare dinosaur. Only seven finds are recorded worldwide, with most of them in Arizona. Even so, its foot size and structure suggests that many Jurassic Period dinosaur trackways in the Southwest—and around the world!— were made by *Dilophosaurus*-like dinosaurs.

Diplodocus
(Dip-plod-oh-cuss)

Dinosaur Group: Diplodocid

Meaning of Name: "Double beam lizard"

Maximum Size: 110 feet long

Lived: 150–145.5 million years ago (Jurassic Period)

Diet: Plants

Discovered: 1877, by Benjamin Mudge and Samuel Wendell Williston; first scientifically described by Othniel Charles Marsh in 1878

Locations in North America: CO, NM, UT, WY

This monster of the Jurassic was the longest dinosaur of North America and one of the largest animals that ever lived on Earth. *Diplodocus* had an extremely long tail, and it featured about 80 vertebrae, an astonishing number by any measure. The tail undoubtedly functioned as a counterweight to its very long neck, but it's supposed

 Fun Facts:

Diplodocus was huge, but it was also sleek and streamlined for its size, weighing in at "only" an estimated 12–18 tons, which is still far more than the largest modern elephant.

that it also doubled as a lethal defensive weapon, whipping back and forth and all around its body. Although many bones and several skeletons of *Diplodocus* have been found, we have scant little skull material to go with them.

Fossils found in these states/provinces

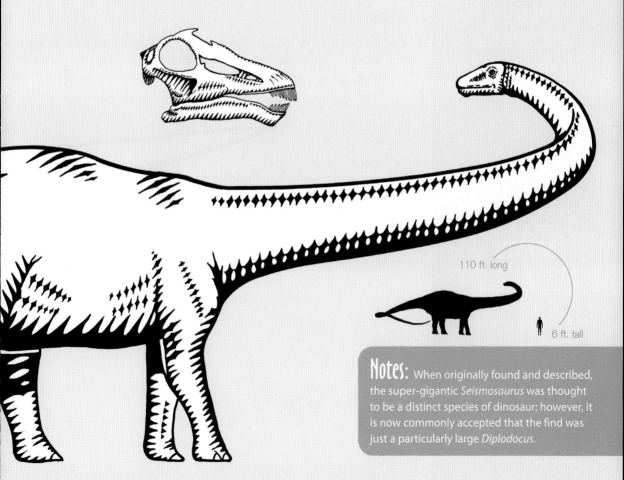

110 ft. long

6 ft. tall

Notes: When originally found and described, the super-gigantic *Seismosaurus* was thought to be a distinct species of dinosaur; however, it is now commonly accepted that the find was just a particularly large *Diplodocus*.

Dromaeosaurus

(Droh-mee-oh-soar-us)

Dinosaur Group: Dromaeosaur

Meaning of Name: "Running lizard"

Maximum Size: 6 feet long

Lived: 76.5–74.8 million years ago (Cretaceous Period)

Diet: Meat

Discovered: 1914, by Barnum Brown; scientifically described by W.D. Matthew and Barnum Brown in 1922

Locations in North America: MT, Alberta

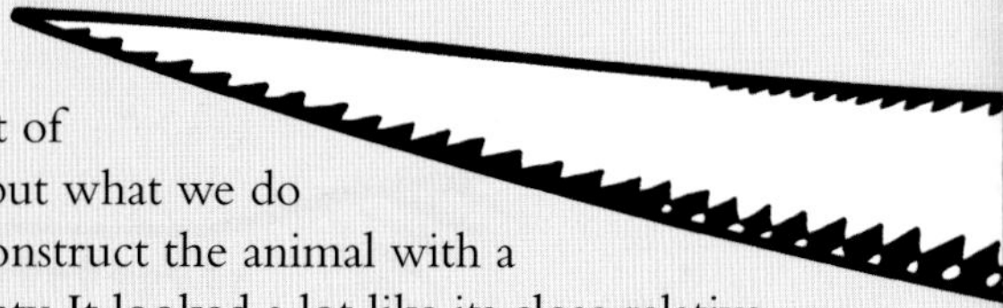

Fun Facts:

Dromaeosaurus had a mouth full of short, tough, sharp teeth. This suggests it could munch, crunch, rip, and tear its meal at will.

We may not have a lot of *Dromaeosaurus* fossils, but what we do have is enough to reconstruct the animal with a good degree of certainty. It looked a lot like its close relative *Deinonychus* but came on the scene much later. The original find and the bulk of *Dromaeosaurus* finds are from the Red Deer River in Alberta's Dinosaur Provincial Park. The stout, lightweight bones of are suggestive of modern birds; consequently, many new reconstructions of *Dromaeosaurus* include feathers.

Notes: Researchers from around the world have suggested that *Dromaeosaurus* were very widespread and that many other finds should be actually classified as *Dromaeosaurus*.

6 ft. long

6 ft. tall

Edmontosaurus

(Ed-mont-uh-soar-us)

Dinosaur Group: Hadrosaur

Meaning of Name: "Edmonton lizard"

Maximum Size: 42 feet long

Lived: 73–66 million years ago (Cretaceous Period)

Diet: Plants

Discovered: 1917, by Lawrence Lambe

Locations in North America: AK, CO, MT, ND, NM, SD, WY, Alberta, Saskatchewan

As perhaps the most prolific dinosaur known, *Edmontosaurus* skeletons grace museum displays around the world. Extensive "bone beds" of this bipedal herbivore have been found in Alberta, Saskatchewan, South Dakota, and Wyoming, and many of these deposits contain a mixture of both young and old animals, indicating *Edmontosaurus* probably lived in large herds and may have been migratory. It was one of the largest hadrosaurs (duck-billed dinosaurs) ever, with a length of up to 42 feet long! Although bipedal, it appears *Edmontosaurus* was able to walk on two legs or four at will.

Fun Facts:

Some *Edmontosaurus* skeletons are so well preserved that skin impressions have been found on them.

Fossils found in these states/provinces

42 ft. long

6 ft. tall

Gorgosaurus

(Gor-go-soar-us)

Dinosaur Group: Tyrannosaur

Meaning of Name: "Terrible lizard"

Maximum Size: 30 feet long

Lived: 76–75 million years ago (Cretaceous Period)

Diet: Meat

Discovered: 1913, by Charles M. Sternberg; scientifically described by Lawrence Lambe in 1914

Locations in North America: Alberta

Those darned tyrannosaurs. It seems like they were everywhere at the end of the Cretaceous. Although *Gorgosaurus* probably lived at the same time and in the same general neighborhood as *Daspletosaurus,* its close tyrannosaur family relative, it appears that they didn't spend much time hanging out together. Researchers think this was due to different living environments—and diets—as seen in many modern animal groups today.

 Fun Facts:

The original excavated specimen of *Gorgosaurus* is one of the most complete finds of this species, and it was the first tyrannosaurid found with a complete set of hand bones.

30 ft. long

6 ft. tall

Notes: Unlike other tyrannosaurids, which are fairly rare, *Gorgosaurus* is known from dozens of specimens and is thus the most well-known member of the tyrannosaur family.

Hadrosaurus

(Had-roh-soar-us)

Dinosaur Group: Hadrosaur

Meaning of Name: "Bulky lizard"

Maximum Size: 32 feet long

Lived: 79 million years ago (Cretaceous Period)

Diet: Plants

Discovered: 1838, by John Estaugh Hopkins; scientifically described by Joseph Leidy in 1858

Locations in North America: NJ

It may surprise you to learn that the North American dinosaur craze didn't begin with *Tyrannosaurus rex*! Instead, it was the discovery of *Hadrosaurus foulkii* in a marl pit near Haddonfield, New Jersey, that really set off dino-mania. Although dinosaurs had been found many years before in Europe, the first bones from our continent were not found until 1858. The specimen became the first mounted dinosaur skeleton in North America and is currently in the collections of the Philadelphia Academy of Natural Sciences.

 **Fun Facts:**

Hadrosaurus foulkii was the first documented dinosaur discovered in North America and is the state fossil of New Jersey.

Fossils found in these states/provinces

32 ft. long

6 ft. tall

Lambeosaurus

(Lam-bee-oh-soar-us)

Dinosaur Group: Hadrosaur

Meaning of Name: "Lambe's lizard"

Maximum Size: 32 feet long

Lived: 76–75 million years ago (Cretaceous Period)

Diet: Plants

Discovered: 1902, by Lawrence Lambe; scientifically described by William Parks in 1923

Locations in North America: Alberta

Lambeosaurus is another dinosaur famous for its ornate crest. Dinosaurs with crests, including the famous double-crested *Dilophosaurus*, appeared first in the Jurassic. And once crests appeared, they diversified fast. *Lambeosaurus* is known for its distinctive cranial crest that some folks say resembles a hatchet. So what was it really used for? Researchers think that the largely hollow crest served a social function (e.g., helping recognize members of their own species), and there is evidence to suggest that the hollow crest was used to "hoot" or communicate with other hadrosaurs.

Fun Facts:

Lambeosaurs had over 100 teeth at any given time and continuously replaced older teeth with new ones throughout their lifetime.

Maiasaura

(My-uh-soar-uh)

Dinosaur Group: Hadrosaur

Meaning of Name: "Good mother lizard"

Maximum Size: 30 feet long

Lived: 76–75 million years ago (Cretaceous Period)

Diet: Plants

Discovered: 1979, by Laurie Trexler; described by Jack Horner and Robert Makela in 1979

Locations in North America: MT

Jack Horner may not have been the first to find dinosaur eggs, but he certainly helped demystify dinosaur parenting behavior as a result of his finds. His original research site—the now-famous Egg Mountain—was populated with a new species of hadrosaur that apparently had a nesting colony. Horner showed that these dinosaurs tended and fed their young while they were in the nest and likely cared for them long after they were born. He therefore gave the newly discovered species a fitting name, *Maiasaura*, which means the "good mother lizard."

 Fun Facts:

Maiasaura hatchlings grew quickly. When hatched, they were just over a foot long, but they were almost five feet long by their first birthday. It's now thought that this high rate of growth is evidence that they were warm-blooded.

Fossils found in these states/provinces

30 ft. long

6 ft. tall

Ornithomimus

(Or-nith-oh-mime-us)

Dinosaur Group: Ornithomimosaur

Meaning of Name: "Bird mimic"

Maximum Size: 12 feet long

Lived: 70-66 million years ago (Cretaceous Period)

Diet: Meat and plants

Discovered: 1889, by George Lyman Cannon; first described by Othniel Charles Marsh in 1890

Locations in North America: CO, MT, NM, SD, TX, UT, WY, Alberta, Saskatchewan

Ornithomimus was a swift, bipedal theropod that had a toothless, bird-like skull and a beak. Because of its similarities to modern-day birds, scientists have postulated that it had an omnivorous diet, as many birds do. Fossils have conclusively shown that some *Ornithomimus* were covered in feathers. It may have had what one might (generously) call wings, but even so, it is generally assumed that *Ornithomimus* couldn't actually fly, although it may have been able to glide.

Fun Facts:

Ornithomimus's leg bones were long, slender and sturdy. This allowed them to be fast and agile in order to escape predators.

Notes: When it comes *Ornithomimus*, there's an ongoing debate about how many species belong to the genus. Even after Dale Russell revamped the classifications in the 1970s, the two primary Ornithomimids—*Struthiomimus* and *Ornithomimus*—still consist of many finds that have a some-what mystifying amount of overlapping characteristics.

Fossils found in these states/provinces

12 ft. long

6 ft. tall

Pachycephalosaurus

(Pack-y-seff-uh-luh-soar-us)

Dinosaur Group: Pachycephalosaur

Meaning of Name: "Thick-headed lizard"

Maximum Size: 15 feet long

Lived: 70–66 million years ago (Cretaceous Period)

Diet: Plants

Discovered: 1860, by Ferdinand Hayden; first scientifically described by Charles Gilmore in 1931

Locations in North America: MT, SD, WY

It's hard to imagine the thick, spiky skullcap of *Pachycephalosaurus* being useful for anything but combat with another bone-headed competitor, and there's no doubt about it, this dinosaur had the thickest skull ever. But some researchers argue that just because you wear a helmet, doesn't mean you engage in fierce combat all the time. That may be true, but it's difficult to think hardware like this was just for show.

Fun Facts:

Pachycephalosaurus may have used its impressive headgear to spar with other members of its species, just like deer and elk do today.

Fossils found in these states/provinces

15 ft. long

6 ft. tall

Parasaurolophus

(Pear-uh-soar-uh-loaf-us)

Dinosaur Group: Hadrosaur

Meaning of Name: "Near-crested lizard"

Maximum Size: 32 feet long

Lived: 76–74 million years ago (Cretaceous Period)

Diet: Plants

Discovered: 1920, by a field party from the University of Toronto; first scientifically described by William Parks in 1922

Locations in North America: MT, NM, UT, Alberta

The long, backward-sweeping crest atop *Parasaurolophus* has confounded paleontologists since the first fossil crest was first found in 1920. Many theories have been advanced about the function of this hollow über-crest. Some argue that it was used for visual display or thermoregulation. One popular theory suggests that the hollow crests were used to communicate. Researchers in New Mexico used high-powered computers to create a digital reproduction of a *Parasaurolophus* crest, and then analyzed what kind of sounds it could produce. One of the *Parasaurolophus* calls produced by the research was long and mournful, similar to a ship's foghorn.

 Fun Facts:

The best, most complete, specimen of *Parasaurolophus* is a juvenile skeleton discovered in 2009. It appears to have been only about one year old when it died.

Notes: *Parasaurolophus*, like most other hadrosaurs, had hundreds of teeth in their mouth at one time. They continually shed and replaced them with new ones as they ate.

Fossils found in these states/provinces

32 ft. long

6 ft. tall

Stegosaurus

(Steg-oh-soar-us)

Dinosaur Group: Stegosaur
Meaning of Name: "Roof lizard"
Maximum Size: 30 feet long
Lived: 155–145 million years ago (Jurassic Period)
Diet: Plants
Discovered: 1877, by Othniel Charles Marsh
Locations in North America: AZ, CO, MT, OK, UT, WY

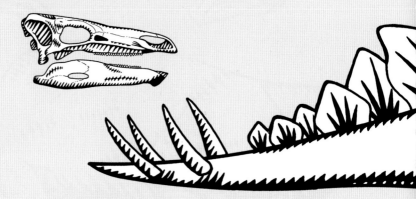

 Fun Facts:

Stegosaurus had a brain about the size of a lime.

One of the Big Five—the five most well-known dinosaurs —*Stegosaurus* was a large herbivorous quadruped. It is one of the most easily recognized of all dinosaurs thanks to the famous plates that run along its back and the imposing spikes at the end of its tail. Large and well-armored, *Stegosaurus* certainly would have been a formidable foe in battle. Although it was a huge quadruped, some researchers suggest *Stegosaurus* could have reared up on its hind legs to browse for higher vegetation, much like large animals do today.

Notes: *Stegosaurus* is famous because of its "armor plates," but their function isn't clear. Some paleontologists suggest they were used for display, while others think they were used for thermoregulation.

Fossils found in these states/provinces

30 ft. long

6 ft. tall

Styracosaurus

(Sty-rack-oh-soar-us)

Dinosaur Group: Ceratopsid

Meaning of Name: "Spiked lizard"

Maximum Size: 18 feet long

Lived: 75 million years ago (Cretaceous)

Diet: Plants

Discovered: 1913, by Charles M. Sternberg; first scientifically described by Lawrence Lambe in 1913

Locations in North America: Alberta

Another in the long and colorful line of ceratopsians (the dino family that includes *Triceratops*), *Styracosaurus* was a big dinosaur with a large, ornate and imposing skull. Like *Triceratops*, it had a large neck frill. But *Styracosaurus* was a little different—it had four to six long horns sticking out of its frill, along with a single large horn on its nose. Like the crests on hadrosaur skulls, the function of the horns on *Styracosaurus* is a matter of much debate.

Fun Facts:

Some *Styracosaurus* had nine horns on their frill and face. The nose horn itself may have reached over two feet long!

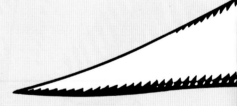

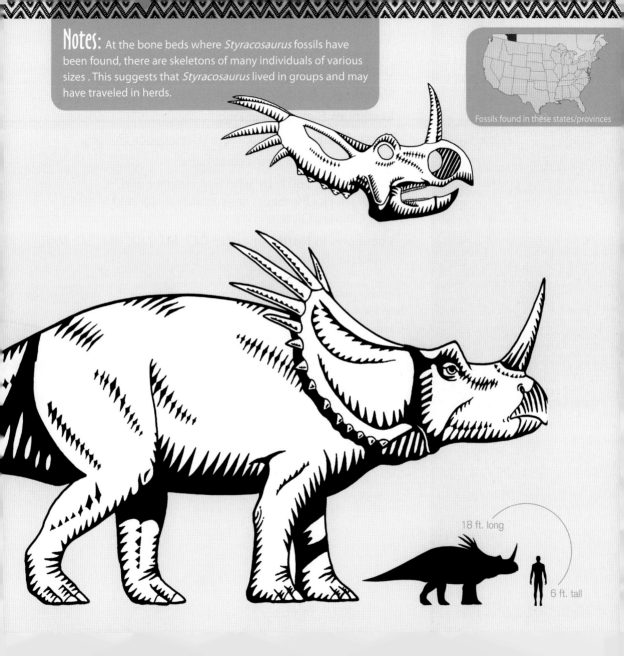

Notes: At the bone beds where *Styracosaurus* fossils have been found, there are skeletons of many individuals of various sizes . This suggests that *Styracosaurus* lived in groups and may have traveled in herds.

Fossils found in these states/provinces

18 ft. long

6 ft. tall

Thescelosaurus

(Theh-sell-oh-soar-us)

 **Fun Facts:**

Several complete *Thescelosaurus* skeletons have been uncovered, making this one of the most well-understood dinosaur anatomies.

Dinosaur Group: Hypsilophodontid

Meaning of Name: "Wonderful lizard"

Maximum Size: 12 feet long

Lived: 70-66 million years ago (Cretaceous Period)

Diet: Suspected to be a plant-eater

Discovered: 1891, by John Bell Hatcher and William H. Utterback; scientifically described in 1913 by Charles Gilmore

Locations in North America: CO, MT, ND, NM, SD, WY, Alberta, Saskatchewan

Thescelosaurus was a bipedal, herbivorous dinosaur that thrived in the late Mesozoic right up until the dinosaur doomsday of the Cretaceous extinction. It's a curious fact that many fine *Thescelosaurus* remains have been recovered from sediments deposited by rivers. Dale Russell studied this and concluded that *Thescelosaurus* lived primarily in floodplains along streams and waterways, and when they died, their bodies were rapidly buried, which preserved the skeletons quite well.

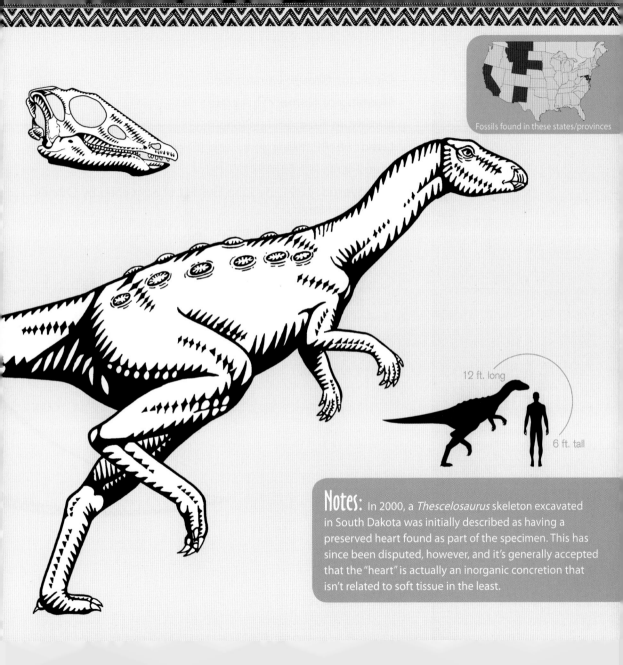

Fossils found in these states/provinces

12 ft. long

6 ft. tall

Notes: In 2000, a *Thescelosaurus* skeleton excavated in South Dakota was initially described as having a preserved heart found as part of the specimen. This has since been disputed, however, and it's generally accepted that the "heart" is actually an inorganic concretion that isn't related to soft tissue in the least.

Torosaurus

(Tore-oh-soar-us)

Dinosaur Group: Ceratopsid

Meaning of Name: "Bull lizard"

Maximum Size: 25 feet long

Lived: 68–66 million years ago (Cretaceous Period)

Diet: Plants

Discovered: 1891, by John Bell Hatcher; named by Othniel Charles Marsh

Locations in North America: CO, MT, ND, SD, TX, UT, WY Saskatchewan

This big-headed monster had a gigantic skull, possibly the largest of any dinosaur. Their skulls alone grew up to ten feet in length and had open areas—often called windows—that were like those of other ceratopsians except *Triceratops*. It's not clear what the purpose of these openings were, but since its discovery *Torosaurus* has certainly attracted attention!

 Fun Facts:

No *Torosaurus* juveniles are known, but a considerable number of *Triceratops* juveniles have been unearthed.

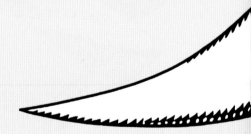

Notes: The similarities and differences between ceratopsian skulls has spawned rigorous debate. Could the differences actually be unique manifestations of the same species? In 2010, paleontologists John Scanella and Jack Horner studied 38 skulls of *Triceratops* and *Torosaurus*. They concluded *Torosaurus* is, in fact, a more mature form of *Triceratops*. Not everyone was convinced, and the debate continues.

Fossils found in these states/provinces

25 ft. long

6 ft. tall

Triceratops
(Tri-sear-uh-tops)

Dinosaur Group: Ceratopsid

Meaning of Name: "Three-horned face"

Maximum Size: 30 feet long

Lived: 68–66 million years ago (Cretaceous Period)

Diet: Plants

Discovered: 1887, by Othniel Charles Marsh

Locations in North America: CO, MT, ND, SD, UT, WY Alberta, Saskatchewan

Another of the "Big Five" most easily recognized dinosaurs, *Triceratops* had a large bony frill and three distinct horns on its huge four-legged body. It's one of the best known of all dinosaurs and for good reason: Several dozen skulls and many complete skeletons have been unearthed, with some finds even including juveniles and subadults. Some specimens have been so well preserved that they have been found with skin impressions.

 Fun Facts:

Although *Triceratops* is often depicted as traveling in herds, there's no real evidence for that assumption.

Fossils found in these states/provinces

30 ft. long

6 ft. tall

Tyrannosaurus
(Tie-ran-oh-soar-us)

Dinosaur Group: Tyrannosaur

Meaning of Name: "Tyrant lizard"

Maximum Size: 42 feet long

Lived: 68–66 million years ago (Cretaceous Period)

Diet: Meat

Discovered: 1874, by Arthur Lakes; scientifically described by Henry Osborn in 1905

Locations in North America: CO, MT, ND, NM, SD, UT, WY, Alberta, Saskatchewan

The king of them all, *Tyrannosaurus rex* is the most recognizable of all dinosaurs. It was a huge and fearsome bipedal carnivore, and its massive skull was full of sharp teeth that were up to 12 inches long. One of the largest predators ever to walk the land, it was an apex predator that preyed upon hadrosaurs, ceratopsians and sauropods. Some researchers have suggested *T. rex* was primarily a scavenger, but this view is not widely accepted.

 Fun Facts:

A complete adult *Tyrannosaurus rex* tooth could be nearly 12 inches long!

Notes: "Sue" is the largest and most complete *Tyrannosaurus rex* known. She (it presumably was female) was found in 1990 by her namesake, Susan Henrickson. It was some find! Sue the dinosaur measures about 40 feet long, weighed up to 8 tons, and was estimated to be about 28 years old when she died. She is now on display at the Field Museum in Chicago.

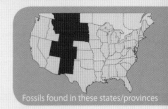

Fossils found in these states/provinces

42 ft. long

6 ft. tall

Non-Dinosaur Fossil Sites in North America

Some of the best fossil sites in North America don't have any dinosaur fossils at all. From Petrified Forest National Park's massive petrified trees to the incredible fossils pulled from the La Brea Tar Pits in Los Angeles, the sheer variety of North America's non-dino fossils boggle the mind. Plus, once you've visited all the dinosaur sites we recommend, visiting these non-dino sites is just the logical next step!

Agate Fossil Beds National Monument

ABOUT THE SITE

You don't need to go to the Serengeti in Africa to see the great diversity of life on the endless savanna. Just go to Nebraska; it's easier! During the Miocene—that's 20 million years ago—the land now known as Agate Fossil Beds National Monument was a grassland comparable to today's Serengeti. It was home to huge pig-like animals, strange camels, compact rhinos, giant beavers and lots more. There were also impressive bear-dogs wandering around trying to figure out whether it was better to be a bear or a dog. The site doesn't have any dinos, but it's just as fun as those that do.

James Cook and Red Cloud

James H. Cook arrived in western Nebraska in the early 1870s while working as a cowboy. He had a keen interest in fossils and had already met the famous paleontologists of the day, Othniel Charles Marsh and Edward Drinker Cope. As the story goes, fossils played a vital role in another, perhaps more important, meeting that he had in 1874 with Lakota Chief Red Cloud. Cook had learned some of the Lakota language and when he met with Red Cloud they apparently talked about rocks and fossils. This chance encounter between Cook and Red Cloud developed into a deep, lasting friendship and Red Cloud visited him often. He often brought gifts for Cook, who proudly displayed them at his ranch house alongside fossils found nearby. The site became a tourist destination, and has been visited by scores of paleontologists over the years. It was established as a National Monument in 1997.

Gift Shop Finds: The park's bookstore, operated by the Oregon Trail Museum Association, features a wide variety of books and products about the park and region.

Location: Harrison, Nebraska.

Type of Site: Museum with old fossil sites nearby.

Age: 20 million years.

Site Rating: ★★★★★

Digging: No digging or collecting. Fully enclosed museum site with self-guided and docent-led tours; the former fossil beds can be visited nearby, as can a series of backcountry hiking trails.

For the Kids: Kids love the life-size displays of the ancient animals, and they can also earn a junior ranger badge in the Junior Ranger program.

Also in the Area: The park is located in the general vicinity of the Nebraska National Forest, which offers camping and hiking opportunities.

Contact Info: www.nps.gov/agfo

From mini rhinos to diminutive camels, this park is the place to learn about the odd mammal life of the Miocene.

More than a few bones!

What's here?
Fossils of *Dinohyus* (a pig-like mammal), *Daphoenodon* (bear-dog), *Menoceras* (a miniature rhinoceros), and *Paleocastor* (an ancient beaver).

Ashfall Fossil Beds State Historical Park

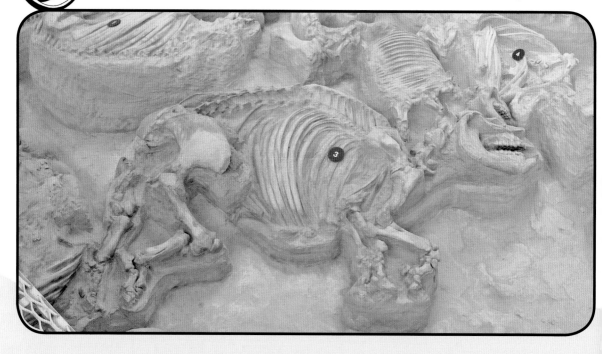

ABOUT THE SITE

Just when you think things are going along quite swimmingly, the Earth erupts in a giant explosion and screws up everything. And I mean everything . . . 12 million years ago the lights went out here amid a humongous volcanic explosion complete with thick clouds of ash. The ash became so thick that the animals of this once-verdant savanna asphyxiated. Horses and rhinos—yes, rhinos!—sought refuge in local watering holes but perished anyway, their bones piling up by the millions. Many were perfectly preserved. Today, you can visit Ashfall Fossil Beds and see the incredible fossils for yourself.

Supervolcano!

What do Yellowstone National Park and Ashfall Fossil Beds have in common? A supervolcano. Yep, Super—with a capital S—much bigger than anything we see today. Scientist have traced the culprit of the Ashfall event to a series of volcanic episodes that are linked directly to Yellowstone. Our beloved first national park sits atop a menacing geologic firebomb that geologists warn will inevitably go off again—hopefully in the very distant future. But, then again, if it weren't for the explosive Ashfall event, we wouldn't have the site's main claim to fame—the incredibly preserved fossils you can see here.

Gift Shop Finds: The park's visitor center features a wide variety of gifts pertaining to dinosaurs, fossils and paleontology, including dinosaur "eggs" that "hatch" dinosaurs when placed in water!

Location: Royal, Nebraska.

Type of Site: A museum with an enclosed bone bed.

Age: 12 million years.

Site Rating: ★★★★★

Digging: No digging or collecting. Fully enclosed site with self-guided and docent-led tours.

For the Kids: The site offers paleodetective activities for kids.

Also in the Area: Check out the famous exhibit known as "Carhenge" located just 3 miles north of Alliance. It's a sculpture of many cars that replicates Stonehenge.

Contact Info:
Open seasonally.
http://ashfall.unl.edu/

It's not all about dinosaurs, people! If you ask me, some of the strange mammal fossils here are just as interesting.

The Hubbard Rhino Barn

What's here?
Fossils of ancient rhinos and horses.

Badlands National Park

ABOUT THE SITE

South Dakota is dinosaur territory, but, alas, there are no actual dinosaur sites here that are open to the public, at least not yet. But it does have the next best thing: Badlands National Park. Oh, sure, there weren't a lot of monster lizards running around, but the fossils found here will astound you nonetheless: rhinos, camels, giant tortoises, saber-toothed cats, gnarly pigs, and lots of other strange creatures from the Oligocene. It's a veritable cornucopia of ancestral mammalian serendipity.

Geology Gone Wild

This is what we call geology in action! You cannot drive, walk, or ride through this park without marveling at the geologic forces hammering away at the sediments deposited here some 60–30 million years ago. The textures and colors are awesome. And so is the visitor center, which has mounted skeletons and an active prep lab where you can see professionals clean and prepare the fossils. The drive through the park has postcard-perfect scenery every mile. Do it at dusk and it becomes Kodachrome. Don't forget your camera!

Gift Shop Finds: The park's excellent bookstore offers everything from replica mammal skulls (that'll definitely liven up your cubicle decor) to park souvenirs for young and old alike. There's even a Badlands National Park Christmas ornament!

Ancient mammals were, well, pretty weird. And Badlands National Park has all sorts of them.

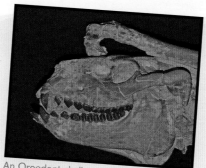

An Oreodont skull

What's here?

Oreodonts (weird pig-like things), giant tortoises, titanotheres (related to both horses and rhinos), and many other fossils.

Location: Wall, South Dakota.

Type of Site: A museum with fossil sites nearby.

Age: 70–30 million years.

Site Rating: ★★★★

Digging: No digging or collecting in the park. Self-guided and ranger led hikes around fossil beds. Local fossils from private land are for sale in Wall and Rapid City.

For the Kids: Wall Drug is loaded with kids' stuff, including rides and dioramas. A prairie dog town is also nearby.

Also in the Area: The famous Wall Drug has good food, singing dummies, a great bookstore, a rock shop, and a zillion tourist attractions. Don't miss it!

Contact Info: www.nps.gov/badl/index.htm

Berlin-Ichthyosaur State Park

ABOUT THE SITE

Berlin-Ichthyosaur State Park was first established in 1957 to protect and display the most abundant concentration of ichthyosaurs—fish-like reptiles—in North America. Ichthyosaurs were ancient marine reptiles that swam in the warm ocean covering central Nevada 225 million years ago. Today, a number of the fossils have been preserved in the Fossil House, which you can tour for a small fee. In addition, the site is also home to the ghost town of Berlin, which features a number of antique buildings, as well as a now-defunct gold mine.

You're Gonna Need a Bigger Boat

It's a very cool thing to be at the top of your game, and that's the way it was for the ichthyosaurs of this state park. Of all the ichthyosaurs world-wide, the ones at Berlin-Ichthyosaur State Park are some of the largest specimens on record, with most being about 50 feet long. Even though they look like huge fish, ichthyosaurs were actually reptiles with eyes that were positively massive in proportion to their bodies. Scientists think they needed these large eyes to hunt in low-light conditions, probably during deep dives in pursuit of prey. What were they after? Well, according to the stomach contents of some ichthyosaurs, the menu often consisted of squid-like creatures.

Gift Shop Finds: There's no gift shop on-site, and the area is pretty remote, so be sure to call ahead before you head out. On occasion, severe weather (especially flash floods) can cause the park to close temporarily.

Location: Austin, Nevada.

Type of Site: A preserved ichthyosaur site and a ghost town.

Age: 225 million years.

Site Rating: ★★★

Digging: No digging or collecting. Self-guided and ranger-led interpretive hikes to fossil deposits.

For the Kids: The Berlin Ghost Town is about as ghost-towny as it gets. Abandoned over 100 years ago, it has several neat buildings and some ancient cars.

Also in the Area: The area is pretty remote, but biking, camping, and picnicking are encouraged and available nearby.

Contact Info: http://parks.nv.gov/parks/bi/

Take a tour of the park's Fossil Shelter to see ichthyosaur fossils, some of them still situated in the ground.

An ichthyosaur at the Fossil Shelter

What's here?
Ichthyosaurs and a ghost town, double the fun!

Florissant Fossil Beds National Monument

ABOUT THE SITE

Once upon a time 35 million years ago, a festive fireworks display got out of hand and had unforeseen consequences. A series of volcanic eruptions spewed out a lot of ugly debris that clogged the local stream valley and consequently flooded the party. The volcanoes kept partying for quite some time, spewing smoking ash and burying wildlife for centuries. These ancient, extra-fine ash sediments preserved the area's wild past, including everything from sequoia stumps the size of delivery trucks to delicate butterflies with their wing patterns preserved. With over 1,700 record species found here, many of them incredibly delicate and rare, Florissant is one of the most important fossil sites on the planet.

Paper Shales

The gentle rolling hills of this valley belies the rich fossil history preserved in paper-thin layers of shale just beneath the grasslands. Florissant's visitor center is a great place to start—it boasts museum displays, a film, bookstore, and some of the greatest fossils in North America. Just outside are some huge fossilized trees. There are also guided tours of fossil excavation sites, as well as a fossil learning lab where you can explore what being a paleontologist is really like. Whatever you do, don't miss the displays of fossilized insects, plants, and even birds at the visitor center. Just south—up the road into the mountains—is the famous historic gold mining district of Cripple Creek with underground tours and a cool historic district.

Gift Shop Finds: The park's bookstore has a great selection of children's books.

In the summer, check out the park's yurt, which is open as a fossil demonstration lab.

Location: Florissant, Colorado.

Type of Site: A museum and fossil sites.

Age: 35 million years.

Site Rating: ★★★★

Digging: You can't collect here. Period. Don't even think of it. Happily, however, you may dig like crazy just south of the Monument at the privately owned Florissant Fossil Quarry. For a small fee, you are outfitted with tools of the trade and are virtually guaranteed to find fossils.

For the Kids: This park offers a junior ranger program and a junior paleontologist program.

Also in the Area: The park isn't far from the fascinating boomtown of Cripple Creek.

Contact Info: www.nps.gov/flfo/index.htm

A fossil insect

What's here?
No dinosaurs, but just about everything else, from fish fossils and incredibly well-preserved insects to plants.

Fossil Butte National Monument

Wyoming is full of dinosaurs, but the state also has some other incredible fossils that any dinosaur hunter would be thrilled to find. Have you ever seen a fossil fish for sale at a rock shop? Chances are, it's from the world-renowned Green River Formation—accumulated sediments from freshwater lakes that covered large parts of Wyoming, Colorado and Utah about 50 million years ago. These incredibly well-preserved fossils are very common in the southwest corner of the state, especially here. In fact, one of these fish, *Knightia eocaena*, has been honored as the state fossil of Wyoming.

Aquarium in Stone

That's what the Park Service informally calls this park, and it's a fitting nickname. The museum at the visitor center has more than 300 fossils on display, the majority of which are fish. There are specimens with scores of small fish on one rock, as well as others with single huge gar fish on a giant table-size slab.

There are all sorts of other fossilized things as well: Every kind of insect you can think of and lots of tropical plants—including palm fronds! Be sure to check out the 13-foot-long crocodile: It might not be a dinosaur, but it's as close as you'll find around these parts!

As with all national parks and monuments, collecting anything in the park borders is against the rules. So leave your shovel and rock pick in the trunk. However, there are private quarries in the area that allow you to dig your own fossil treasure—for a fee, of course. Our favorite is also one of the oldest: Warfield Fossil Safari (www.fossilsafari.com).

Gift Shop Finds: The National Monument operates a small bookstore, where you can purchase books and other media about the amazing fossils and history of Fossil Butte.

Location: Kemmerer, Wyoming.

Type of Site: World-famous Green River Formation fossils, a museum and trails.

Age: 50 million years.

Site Rating: ★★★★★

Digging: No digging is allowed in the Monument, but there are a few private fish quarries outside the park near Kemmerer; there, you can pay to dig and keep what you find.

For the Kids: The park offers a Junior Ranger program for kids.

Also in the Area: Warfield Fossil Safari is our favorite pay-to-dig site, though do not visit the area in inclement weather.

Contact Info:
Fossil Butte:
www.nps.gov/fobu/index.htm

Warfield Fossil Safari:
www.fossilsafari.com

Head here to see more fossil fish than you shake a stick at!

Gone fishing! Digging fish from 50 million years ago.

What's here?
Fossil fish, stingrays, plants, and even insects.

George Page Museum La Brea Tar Pits

ABOUT THE SITE

Los Angeles hasn't always been covered in smog. A short 400 centuries ago it was a thriving savanna teeming with life, including everything from the world-famous saber-toothed tigers and dire wolves to outright odd creatures such as giant sloths. We know about all this life thanks to something of a geological quirk—the area is home to deposits of asphalt, which, like the familiar material used to surface driveways, is thick and gooey. Over time, animals became trapped in the pits, which then attracted predators, some of whom were also trapped. All of these remains piled up in bone beds and became preserved. In all, over a million bones are estimated to have been deposited here, and excavations are still ongoing today, over a century since the first discoveries.

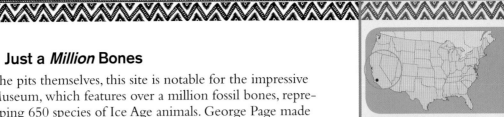

No Big Deal, Just a *Million* Bones

In addition to the pits themselves, this site is notable for the impressive George Page Museum, which features over a million fossil bones, representing a whopping 650 species of Ice Age animals. George Page made his fortune in gift baskets. (It's true, he pioneered the now-ubiquitous fruit- and gift-basket business.) Seeing the educational potential of this site, he donated the money to preserve it. Perhaps the craziest thing about this place, which is clearly one of the greatest fossil sites ever discovered, is its location right in the middle of downtown Los Angeles. Of course, at the time these animals were out and about, the area was a little less crowded and didn't have any public transportation.

Gift Shop Finds: The park offers fossil replicas, toys, and even little display stands that feature 3D-printed skulls of some of the animals found on-site. (Oddly, these also double as necklaces, though we're not sure what we think of that.)

You've seen the La Brea Tar Pits in movies, now see it up close!

Smilodon

Location: Los Angeles, California.

Type of Site: A museum with enclosed tar pits, bone beds and tar seeps.

Age: 40,000 years.

Site Rating: ★★★★★

Digging: The Natural History Museum of Los Angeles County has a long list of opportunities near and far, for members, visitors, and guests.

For the Kids: The site offers a number of special museum events geared toward kids.

Also in the Area: Being in downtown L.A. means you have your pick of cool things in the city and along the shore. There's way too much to even list.

Contact Info:
www.tarpits.org

L.A. Natural History Museum:
www.nhm.org/site/activities-programs

What's here?
Fossils of dire wolves, saber-toothed cats, mammoths, horses, giant sloths, birds, and even insects.

John Day Fossil Beds National Monument

ABOUT THE SITE

John Day Fossil Beds National Monument is one of the greatest geological and paleontological preserves on Earth. Consisting of three separate land units, the fossil record here spans an incredible 41 million years, covering most of the Cenozoic Era, aka the "Age of Mammals." So can you guess what kind of fossils you'll find here? Well, they aren't dinosaurs! Over millions of years, the area was home to all kinds of incredible mammals: from primitive rhinos and three-toed horses, to saber-toothed cats and huge short-faced bears. And those are just a start! The Monument is also home to the famous Painted Hills, which are aptly named. Long story short: A visit is well worth the trip even if there aren't any dinosaurs!

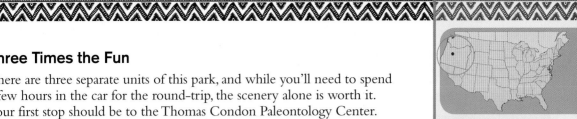

Three Times the Fun

There are three separate units of this park, and while you'll need to spend a few hours in the car for the round-trip, the scenery alone is worth it. Your first stop should be to the Thomas Condon Paleontology Center. Here, you'll find displays of fossils from all three portions of the park. The center also features a working fossil lab that has a huge window, giving you the chance to watch scientists work on real fossils from the Monument. Even though the site has been the subject of dedicated research for over a century, new discoveries continue to be made. If you want to see fossils up close and personal, you can take the "Trail of Fossils" at the Clarno unit. There, you can see fossils weathering out of the rock. But don't touch!— disturbing them is prohibited.

Gift Shop Finds: The Sheep Rock Unit of the park operates a bookstore at the Thomas Condon Paleontology Center.

From the park's paleontology to the Painted Hills, this is a place to savor!

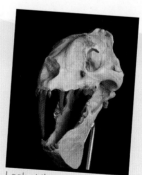

Look at those teeth!

What's here?
Miocene mammals and petrified wood.

Location: Bend, Oregon.

Type of Site: A museum and Cenozoic mammal fossil beds.

Age: 40–10 million years.

Site Rating: ★★★★★

Digging: The park's volunteers sometimes assist researchers and scientists in digs.

For the Kids: This park offers a number of educational programs for kids, many led by the Monument's paleontology staff.

Also in the Area: Mount Bachelor ski resort brings in skiers from all over. Bend is also near the Cascade Lakes, which are a large draw for tourists.

Contact Info: www.nps.gov/joda/index

Mammoth Site of Hot Springs

ABOUT THE SITE

About 26,000 years ago, things got a little dramatic in Hot Springs. The roof of a sinkhole cavern suddenly collapsed, creating a spring-fed pond with abrupt sides. The warm waters attracted local wildlife, including mammoths. Getting into the pond was no problem, but getting out was another matter. Unfortunately, the steep, slippery sides could not be negotiated by the mammoths and many died as a result. Their bones piled up and their skeletons fossilized in the accumulating sediments. Fast-forward a couple dozen millennia and along comes a developer wanting to build a subdivision. George "Porky" Hansen was an equipment operator, and his son, Dan, was really into rocks. One day in 1974 Porky's bulldozer kicked up some strange-looking items, and Dan recognized one as being a mammoth tooth. That was the start of the Mammoth Site.

A Mammoth Amount of Mammoths

With a name like "Mammoth Site" you expect to find mammoths, and this place doesn't disappoint. In fact, a total of 61 mammoths have been found here so far. Columbian mammoths make up the majority, but a few woolly mammoths are thrown in to round out the mix. You can see many of the fossils as they looked when they were discovered—they are preserved in situ in the ground. The site is now protected by a building that encloses the bone bed with walkways running through several sections, enabling visitors to get a good close look at the diggings. And even though the site is famous for mammoths, dozens of other fossils have been discovered here, including short-faced bears, prairie dogs, wolves, plants, and even a fish or two.

In addition to the fossils, the site also features a full-size recreated Paleolithic mammoth bone hut that you can walk through, replica mounts of mammoths, hands-on exhibits, and much more!

Gift Shop Finds: In addition to a wide variety of books, DVDs and other items, the site also offers replica fossils, including everything from replica mammoth tusks and teeth to replicas of short-faced bear skulls.

Don't miss the full-size mammoth model; kids love it.

A full mammoth skeleton

Location: Hot Springs, South Dakota.

Type of Site: A museum with an enclosed mammoth bone bed.

Age: 26,000 years.

Site Rating: ★★★★★

Digging: No digging or collecting. Fully enclosed site with self-guided and docent-led tours.

For the Kids: The site offers a number of junior paleontologist programs where kids will dig for replica fossils; the site even offers a spear-throwing class, where kids can (safely) wield an atlatl, an ancient weapon.

Also in the Area: You are very near Custer State Park, so take the kids out to see real buffalo in their native environment.

Contact Info: http://mammothsite.com/

What's here?
Columbian mammoths and woolly mammoths in a unique pileup of bones.

Mastodon State Historic Site

ABOUT THE SITE

So, what's the difference between a mastodon and a mammoth? While they look alike, they are not closely related. Mammoths are close relatives of current-day elephants and first appeared around 5 million years ago. Mastodons are more distantly related and first appeared around 27 million years ago. So guess what they found at Mastodon Historic Site? (Hint—it was not a mammoth!) The mastodon bones discovered here are important because they were found in association with human artifacts, providing the first direct proof that people lived alongside—and may have hunted—these ancient proboscideans. But while it is accepted that humans ate mammoth and mastodon meat, the theory of humans actively hunting the giant beasts is hotly debated.

Meet the Clovis People

First, the bad news: You won't see any real fossil digging here. While many important fossils were indeed found here, the bone beds have been reburied to protect them until future excavations are carried out. (When the bone beds were exposed, they were subjected to quite a bit of theft and vandalism.) But that doesn't mean the site isn't worth visiting; on the contrary, the museum does a fine job of interpreting the intertwined fates of mastodons and the Clovis culture, the ancient American Indians who once lived here between 10,000 and 14,000 years ago. The park's interpretive trails give you an option to learn more while out and about, and the picnic sites also offer great spots to relax once you're through with the museum and trails.

Gift Shop Finds: If you're interested in learning more about the park's past or the Clovis People, check out the park's bookstore for a variety of options.

Location: Imperial, Missouri.

Type of Site: A museum and an inactive bone bed site.

Age: 12,000 years.

Site Rating: ★★⯨

Digging: No digging or collecting.

For the Kids: This is one of the smaller units in the large Missouri state parks system. There are occasionally park events geared for kids.

Also in the Area: You are not far from St. Louis with a ton of attractions, including the world-famous Gateway Arch.

Contact Info: https://mostateparks.com/park/mastodon-state-historic-site

The museum has some great displays about the Clovis People and their relationship with mastodons.

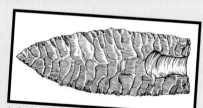

A Clovis projectile point

What's here?
A recreation of a scene that features Clovis people and mastodons.

U-Dig Fossils

ABOUT THE SITE

Located about an hour west of Delta, Utah, the U-Dig quarry is the place to go if you want to find trilobites. Trilobites, which became extinct before the Age of Dinosaurs, were oceanic arthropods related to present-day spiders and scorpions. At the U-Dig site, zillions of trilobites were buried in the deep, dark muds of an ancient sea. Here you find direct evidence of what scientists call the "Cambrian Explosion," a period in time when life on Earth diversified very quickly. Trilobite populations, in particular, went bananas, and they ruled the Earth for many millions of years.

Way Older than Dinosaurs

Trilobites have seniority! Maybe we're going a little off the dinosaur track here, but you're gonna love it! Compared to trilobites, dinosaurs are young pups. Trilobites rose to prominence over 500 million years ago. They aren't just older than dinosaurs, they're older than all terrestrial life. Yep—life on land started some 100 million years after these guys started swimming around the oceans. Looking something like a cross between a horseshoe crab and a space alien, trilobites are an unforgettable find. And given how many of them are in the Wheeler Shale exposures of U-dig's quarry, you'll find plenty. We guarantee it! You can also find other fossils here, too—including sponges and brachiopods—but the trilobites are the stars of the show.

Gift Shop Finds: If you can't make it to the quarry, you can have the quarry shipped to you! For about $90, the quarry will send you a 40-pound chunk of trilobite-rich slate along with instructions on how to find fossils in it. For details, visit their website.

If you want to find fossils yourself, head here. You'll find plenty!

Location: Delta, Utah.

Type of Site: A famous trilobite dig site that is open to the public.

Age: 500 million years.

Site Rating: ★★★★

Digging: Pay to dig and keep all you find. And you will find plenty!

For the Kids: Special rates for kids and teenagers. Schools groups welcome at a special discount.

Also in the Area: You might think you're in the middle of nowhere, but the fact is you're near some really cool places. Top of the list is Great Basin National Park to the west.

Contact Info:
www.u-digfossils.com

A trilobite find

> **What's here?**
> Cambrian trilobites that you dig yourself.

Waco Mammoth National Monument

ABOUT THE SITE

On a fine spring day in 1978, Paul Barron and Eddie Bufkin embarked on a search for arrowheads and fossils near the Bosque River. They soon stumbled upon something else altogether: a very large bone eroding out of a ravine. They took the bone to the Strecker Museum at nearby Baylor University, where it was examined and identified as the femur of a Columbian mammoth (*Mammuthus columbi*). The museum organized a team to search for more bones, and digging soon began. This paleontology party hasn't stopped; since then, scientists have found 19 mammoths. Today, the dig site is now enclosed and climate controlled, and it was recently named a National Monument.

A River of Mammoths

When you stare down from the elevated walkway at all the bones below you'll ask yourself: How did this happen? It's a bit different than the Mammoth Site in South Dakota (page 146). There was no big hole in the ground filled with spring water that attracted mammoths, which got stuck in the pit, then died. Instead, research indicates these animals were caught in a very sudden geologic event—like a flood or landslide—and were quickly buried in the process. Every size and age of mammoths are jammed together: mothers, fathers, and youngsters were overwhelmed and suddenly entombed in the sediments. Most of the bones found at this site are preserved in situ (left in place in the ground, just as they were found), and research on them continues. The walkway gives you a bird's-eye view of the whole scene. By the way, mammoths are not the only fossils found here; there are also camels (yes, camels!) and saber-toothed cats.

Gift Shop Finds: There's no gift shop on-site, but the Monument is located in Waco, a thriving city of more than 130,000 people, so shopping opportunities abound.

Location: Waco, Texas.

Type of Site: A famous enclosed bone bed of mammoths.

Age: 65,000 years.

Site Rating: ★★★★

Digging: Sorry, not here!

For the Kids: The National Monument offers special educational classes for kids, including "Fossil Fun," a $3 add-on program where you can sort through fossil-rich gravel and keep what you find.

Also in the Area: Waco has loads of attractions, including the Dr. Pepper Museum and the Texas Ranger Hall of Fame.

Contact Info: www.nps.gov/waco/

The Dig Center's elevated walkway gives you a bird's-eye view of the bone bed.

Just a few of the bones on-site

What's here?
Columbian mammoths inside a large climate-controlled building.

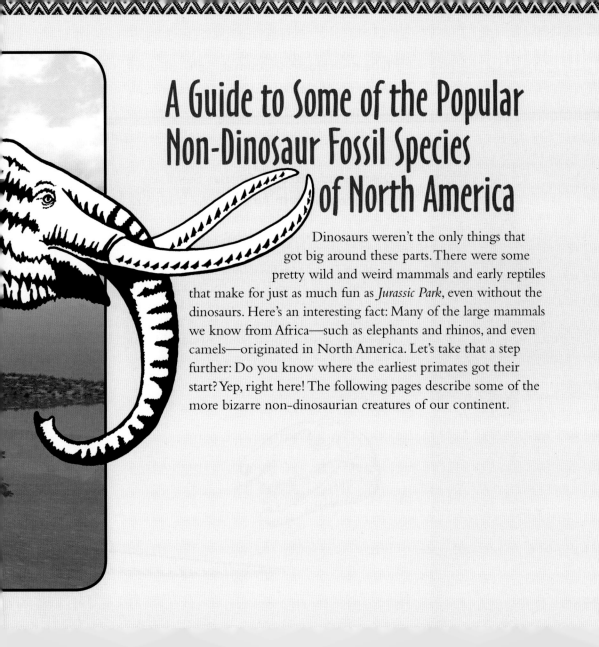

A Guide to Some of the Popular Non-Dinosaur Fossil Species of North America

Dinosaurs weren't the only things that got big around these parts. There were some pretty wild and weird mammals and early reptiles that make for just as much fun as *Jurassic Park*, even without the dinosaurs. Here's an interesting fact: Many of the large mammals we know from Africa—such as elephants and rhinos, and even camels—originated in North America. Let's take that a step further: Do you know where the earliest primates got their start? Yep, right here! The following pages describe some of the more bizarre non-dinosaurian creatures of our continent.

Dimetrodon

(Die-meet-tra-don)

Type of Prehistoric Animal: Sphenacodont

Meaning of Name: "Two measures of teeth"

Maximum Size: 15 feet long

Lived: 290–272 million years ago (Permian Period)

Diet: Meat

Discovered: 1878, by Charles Sternberg

Locations in North America: AZ, NM, OK, TX, UT

This four-legged predator of the early Permian wasn't a dinosaur, even though it's often described as such in books, movies and popular culture. *Dimetrodon* lived long before the first dinosaurs appeared and belongs to a group known confusingly as "mammal-like reptiles." Long story short: It's more closely related to mammals than reptiles, but it's not an ancestor of either . . . go figure. Dinosaur or not, they were some awesome-looking creatures!

 **Fun Facts:**

Even though it's often mistaken for one, *Dimetrodon* wasn't a dinosaur.

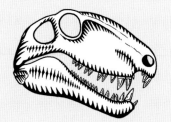

Fossils found in these states/provinces

Notes: *Dimetrodon* is famous for its sail-like back. But the exact function of the "sail" is not understood. It could have been for display or used for thermo-regulation of its body temperature.

15 ft. long

6 ft. tall

Dire Wolf

Type of Prehistoric Animal: Dire wolf

Meaning of Name: "Fearsome dog"

Maximum Size: 5 feet long

Lived: 250,000–10,000 years ago (Pleistocene Epoch)

Diet: Meat

Discovered: 1854, by Francis A. Linck; scientifically described by Joseph Leidy in 1858

Locations in North America: Widespread in North America

The dire wolf—*Canis dirus*—was, as the name implies, a formidable predator, and very abundant in the late Ice Age. As a result, it's one of most common finds in the La Brea Tar Pits (see page 142). *Canis dirus* first appeared in North America, later spreading into South America. It's not precisely clear why dire wolves went extinct, but pressure from a changing climate is thought to have played a role.

 Fun Facts:

The dire wolf was the largest member of the genus *Canis*, which includes modern dogs. It weighed up to 175 pounds!

At the end of the Pleistocene, about 10,000 years ago, a large extinction event occurred, wiping out many of the larger animals in North America. Even though the dire wolf was very abundant and had been incredibly successful up to that point, it too disappeared.

Widespread in North America

5 ft. long

6 ft. tall

Daphoenodon

(Daff-fen-oh-don)

Type of Prehistoric Animal: Bear-dog
Meaning of Name: "Blood-reeking tooth"
Maximum Size: Perhaps 8 feet long
Lived: 40 million years ago to 10,000 years ago (Cenozoic Era)
Diet: Meat and plants
Discovered: 1908, by T.F. Olcott
Locations in North America: Widespread in North America

Is it a bear or a dog? Well, both and neither. *Daphoenodon* is a member of the Amphicyonids, or "bear–dogs." If you want to picture what seeing one in the wild would look like, imagine a cross between a tough dog (say, a pit bull) and an American black bear. Needless to say, no thanks!

Fun Facts:

Although bear-dogs spanned almost 40 million years of evolution, they died out in the Pleistocene extinctions.

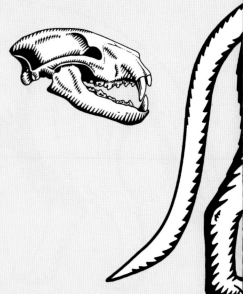

In addition to their appearance, bear-dogs get their name because of the traits that they share with both bears and dogs, including the tendency to construct dens. In fact, a fossilized bear-dog den was even discovered at Agate Fossil Beds National Monument (page 130); the site even included cached food that the bear-dog was planning on eating later.

Widespread in North America

8 ft. long

6 ft. tall

Eohippus

(Ee-oh-hip-us)

Type of Prehistoric Animal: Horse ancestor

Meaning of Name: "Dawn horse"

Maximum Size: 4 feet long

Lived: 56–50 million years ago (Eocene Epoch)

Diet: Plants

Discovered: 1876, by Othniel Charles Marsh

Locations in North America: Widespread in North America

Do you have a horse-crazed member of your family? Well, they'd have loved to own one of these diminutive ancestors of the modern-day horse. At only two to three feet tall, *Eohippus* would have made an irresistible pet, and parents everywhere would no doubt have to deal with the inevitable demands for one when birthdays and Christmas came around. (And that doesn't even mention how difficult it probably would be to house-train a prehistoric horse.) So maybe it's a good thing they went extinct ...

 **Fun Facts:**

Eohippus is the earliest known ancestor of the modern horse.

Notes: Unlike modern horses, *Eohippus* had multiple toes on each foot, which supported its legs. Over time, however, they evolved to rely on a single toe and a single hoof, as we see in modern horses today.

Widespread in North America

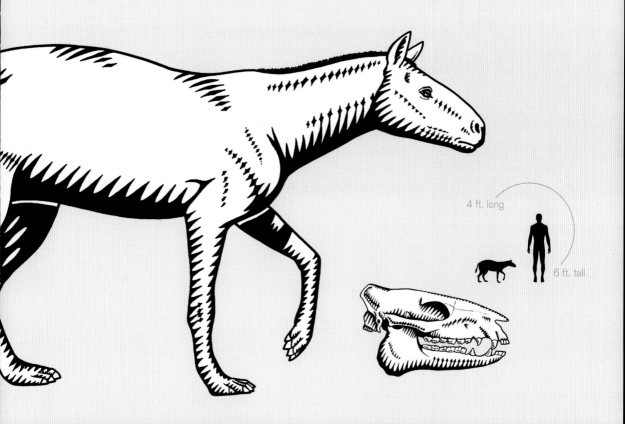

4 ft. long

6 ft. tall

Ichthyosaurs

(Ick-thea-oh-saurs)

Type of Prehistoric Animal: Marine reptile

Meaning of Name: "Fish lizard"

Maximum Size: 60 feet long

Lived: 250–90 million years ago
(Triassic, Jurassic and Cretaceous Periods)

Diet: Meat

Discovered: 1811, by Mary Anning; scientifically
described by Charles Koenig in 1819

Locations in North America: AK, CA, ND, NV

There is definitely something fishy about ichthyosaurs. After all, they looked a lot like big fish, but they weren't really fish at all. Instead, they were reptiles that lived in the seas during the Age of Dinosaurs. Like other reptiles, ichthyosaurs had to surface to breathe air. Nonetheless, they hunted like sharks; their fish-like shape was a helpful adaptation that allowed them to move more effectively in water. Ichthyosaurs are also notable for their uncommonly large eyes that no doubt helped them hunt prey far below the ocean's surface.

 **Fun Facts:**

Not closely related to dinosaurs, ichthyosaurs looked and acted more like an early shark.

60 ft. long

6 ft. tall

Notes: Upon learning that ichthyosaurs were actually seagoing reptiles, one of the first questions paleontologists had was, "Well how did they give birth?" Today's aquatic reptiles, such as the sea turtle, return to the land to lay eggs. But fossil evidence shows that ichthyosaurs gave birth to live young in the water.

Megatherium

(Mega-theer-ee-um)

Type of Prehistoric Animal: Giant sloth

Meaning of Name: "Great beast"

Maximum Size: 20 feet long

Lived: 6 million years ago to 10,000 years ago (Quaternary Period)

Diet: Plants

Discovered: 1788, by Manuel Torres; described by Georges Cuiver in 1796

Locations in North America: Widespread in North America

Megatherium, also known as the giant ground sloth, was no Tiny Tim. It is thought to have weighed as much as four tons or nearly as much as two cars. *Megatherium* had a gnarly, robust skeleton with fat, stocky bones to support its immense size. Despite its colossal rotundity, it seems *Megatherium* was able to stand on its hind legs and forage into trees much higher than other animals of its time.

Fun Facts:

It may have been slow, but it seems like no predators cared to dine on *Megatherium* meat, so why hurry?

Notes: Like modern anteaters, *Megatherium* had a curious gait: It walked on the sides of its feet, sort of rolling them underneath. Walking like this was a necessity because its large claws prevented it from putting its feet flat on the ground.

Widespread in North America

20 ft. long

6 ft. tall

Mastodon

(Mast-oh-don)

Type of Prehistoric Animal: Mastodon

Meaning of Name: "Breast tooth"

Maximum Size: 12 feet tall

Lived: 1.8 million years ago to 10,000 years ago (Pliocene Epoch to Quaternary Period)

Diet: Plants

Discovered: 1705, by a farmer in Claverack, NY; described by Robert Kerr in 1792

Locations in North America: Widespread in North America

As you might expect from their appearance, mastodons are somewhat related to elephants. Their evolution paralleled that of mammoths, another proboscidean (elephant relative) with whom they share a common ancestor. Mastodons and mammoths coexisted in many of the same environments, but it doesn't appear there was any conflict between the two groups, probably because they ate different plants. Alas, these magnificent creatures disappeared from North America as part of the mass extinction that wiped out most of the Pleistocene megafauna.

 Fun Facts:

Mastodons and mammoths coexisted for thousands of years, but both became extinct at the end of the Pleistocene.

Widespread in North America

12 ft. tall

6 ft. tall

Mammoth

(Mam-muth)

Type of Prehistoric Animal: Mammoth

Meaning of Name: "Mammon's horn"

Maximum Size: 13 feet tall

Lived: 5 million years ago to 10,000 years ago
(Pliocene Epoch to Quaternary Period)

Diet: Plants

Discovered: 1722, by John Bell, first scientifically described
by Joshua Brookes in 1828

Locations in North America: Widespread in North America

Woolly mammoths (*Mammuthus primigenius*) are the most famous
mammoths of North America. Belonging to a group known as
proboscideans (which includes elephants and their relatives),
their ancestors began evolving nearly 55 million years ago.
The typical Ice Age mammoths appeared much more
recently, about 5 million years ago. Mammoths and mastodons
coexisted with early humans during the Ice Age, and it's a
well-known fact that Paleoindians ate their meat.

Fun Facts:

The mammoth's closest living
relative is the Asian elephant.

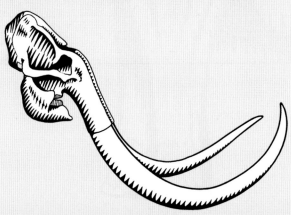

Notes: The Hebior Mammoth, found in a Wisconsin cornfield, is the biggest and most complete woolly mammoth ever excavated in North America. It was killed and butchered by Paleoindians about 12,500 years ago. Although the mammoth may be extinct, some groups have an idea to change that; they've announced plans to "de-extinct" mammoths and other animals via cloning. The big debate is whether this is right or wrong. What do you think?

Widespread in North America

13 ft. tall

6 ft. tall

Megacerops
(Mega-sear-ops)

Type of Prehistoric Animal: Brontothere

Meaning of Name: "Large horn face"

Maximum Size: 18 feet long

Lived: 38–34 million years ago (Eocene Epoch)

Diet: Plants

Discovered: 1870, by Joseph Leidy

Locations in North America: CO, MT, NE, SD, WY

Brontotheres were a group of large mammals that flourished during most of the Eocene. *Megacerops* is one of the most well-known genera of these creatures, which were something like a cross between a horse and a rhinoceros. However you describe them, they grew very large before they went extinct rather suddenly about 34 million years ago. Thankfully, they left behind an excellent fossil record in North America, and they're especially well represented in the Badlands of South Dakota.

 **Fun Facts:**

The earliest brontotheres were fairly small, but as they evolved they developed massive bodies and a great deal of ornamentation on their nose, as typified by *Megacerops*.

Fossils found in these states/provinces

18 ft. long

6 ft. tall

Notes: Although they may have looked like gnarly rhinos, brontotheres are actually more closely related to horses. That'd be some really huge, weird horses.

Menoceras

(Me-no-sear-us)

Type of Prehistoric Animal: Rhino

Meaning of Name: "Crescent horns"

Maximum Size: 5 feet long

Lived: 31–20 million years ago (Oligocene and Miocene Epochs)

Diet: Plants

Discovered: 1921, by E.L. Troxell

Locations in North America: Widespread in North America

Have you ever wanted a small pet rhino? Well, *Menoceras* would fit the bill. They lived during the Oligocene and the Miocene and stood only about three to four feet tall. What they lacked in stature they made up in numbers, as they were pretty prolific, and ranged as far south as Central America.

 Fun Facts:

Not all *Menoceras* had horns; males had horns, but females were hornless.

Widespread in North America

5 ft. long

6 ft. tall

Merycoidodon

(Mare-eee-coy-doe-dawn)

Type of Prehistoric Animal: Oreodont

Meaning of Name: "Ruminating teeth"

Maximum Size: 6 feet long

Lived: 38–16 million years ago (Eocene and Miocene Epochs)

Diet: Plants

Discovered: 1848, by Joseph Leidy

Locations in North America: Widespread in North America

Originally it was thought that oreodonts like *Merycoidodon* were related to pigs and peccaries. But later some researchers said they were more closely related to camels. Now everyone's confused by the whole shebang. Maybe we can settle it with taking a page from the *Daphoenodon* (page 160) book and call it a "pig-camel"? But somehow that doesn't seem to have a ring to it, like "bear-dog" does . . .

 Fun Facts:

Merycoidodon looked a lot like sheep but that doesn't mean they were fast on their feet. In fact, given the way their bones were constructed, it's unlikely that *Merycoidodon* could run very fast at all.

Widespread in North America

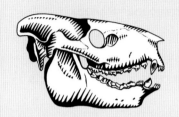

6 ft. long

6 ft. tall

Mosasaurs
(Mose-uh-soars)

Type of Prehistoric Animal: Marine reptile

Meaning of Name: "Meuse river lizard"

Maximum Size: 50 feet long

Lived: 92–66 million years ago (Cretaceous Period)

Diet: Meat

Discovered: 1764, by quarry workers in the Netherlands

Locations in North America: Several U.S. states, Canada

While *Tyrannosaurus rex* stomped around on land terrorizing the neighborhood, mosasaurs were scaring the bejeezus out of ammonites and squids in the oceans of the late Mesozoic. These large, powerful swimmers were the top-dog predators of their environment. Although they might resemble the sea monsters once shown on antique maps, mosasaurs were real marine monsters in their own right. These gnarly reptiles grew to the hellaceous length of 50 feet, possibly even more.

 **Fun Facts:**

The smallest-known mosasaur is *Dallasaurus*. Can you guess where they found that one? It was only about three feet long.

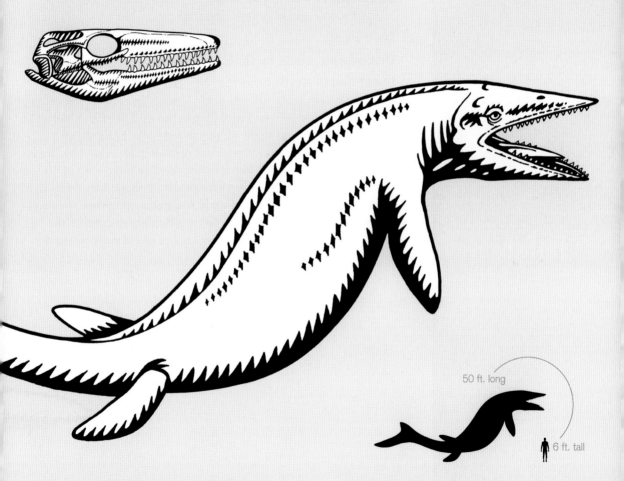

Notes: Direct descendants of land-dwelling reptiles, a mosasaur's flippers were highly adapted versions of a terrestrial reptile's front and hind feet. These fins, in combination with their large, strong tail, made a mosasaur a highly mobile predator, ensuring their success against prey such as ammonites, turtles, fish, and squid.

Widespread in North America

50 ft. long

6 ft. tall

Palaeocastor

(Pale-lee-oh-cast-or)

Type of Prehistoric Animal: Beaver

Meaning of Name: "Prehistoric beaver"

Maximum Size: 2 feet long

Lived: 25–18 million years ago
(Oligocene and Miocene Epochs)

Diet: Plants

Discovered: 1892, by Dr. E.H. Barbour

Locations in North America: NE, SD

It was a classic case of whodunit: Out in the middle of the Nebraska ranchlands, folks found these weird, curved rock features they nicknamed "Devil's Corkscrews." But nobody had a clue how they were formed. These screw-like formations were huge—up to 10 feet tall—and confounded scientists who originally described them as giant freshwater sponges. Later, some researchers proposed they were fossil plants. The mystery wasn't solved until they discovered the skeleton of a fossilized beaver—now known as *Palaeocastor*—in the base of a "Devil's Corkscrew."

Fun Facts:

Palaeocastor dug its unique corkscrew-shaped burrows with its teeth, not its claws!

Notes: When the weird "Devil's Corkscrews" were first discovered, scientists were at a loss, and many different explanations were proposed. One early theory even speculated the strange structures were created by two plants that became intertwined, winding again and again around one another, creating the corkscrew pattern.

2 ft. long

6 ft. tall

Plesiosaurs
(Please-ee-uh-soars)

Type of Prehistoric Animal: Marine reptile

Meaning of Name: "Near-to lizard"

Maximum Size: 50 feet long

Lived: 203–66 million years ago
(Triassic and Cretaceous Periods)

Diet: Fish and shellfish

Discovered: 1605, by Richard Verstegen; first described by
Henry de la Beche and William Conybeare in 1821

Locations in North America: KS

As if ichthyosaurs and mosasaurs were not enough, along come
plesiosaurs to swell the ranks of marine reptiles even further. This
huge group of antediluvian monsters had short tails, long necks, and
large, robust flippers for swimming. The fossil record of plesiosaurs
is positively littered with finds; since *Plesiosaurus* was first named in
1821, more than a hundred species have been described.

 **Fun Facts:**

Like other marine reptiles of the
day, plesiosaurs breathed air
and bore live young.

Fossils found in these states/provinces

50 ft. long

6 ft. tall

Notes: Although bones of plesiosaurs have been found as far back as the 1500s, they were considered such an enigma that it took hundreds of years to describe them scientifically. They weren't considered a distinct group of fossil animals until 1821.

Pterosaurs

(Tear-oh-soars)

Type of Prehistoric Animal: Flying reptile

Meaning of Name: "Flying reptile"

Maximum Size: 36 feet wingspan

Lived: 228–66 million years ago
(from the Triassic to the Cretaceous Period)

Diet: Varied

Discovered: 1784, by Cosimo Alessandro Collini

Locations in North America: Widespread in North America

Well, it's about time we got off the marine reptile kick and started in on something entirely different, like flying reptiles! Just like the marine reptiles, however, pterosaurs were *not* dinosaurs. But they were reptiles, and highly specialized ones at that, as their appendages had adapted to help them achieve flight. Their bones were long, strong and hollow, like those of birds. They also had large, robust breastbones where their wing muscles attached. All in all, pterosaurs are a huge group, and individual species varied accordingly. Some pterosaurs, such as *Pteryodactylus*, had long jaws full of teeth. Others, such as the famous *Pteranodon*, were toothless.

 Fun Facts:

Pterosaurs were the very first vertebrate animals to achieve powered flight.

Widespread in North America

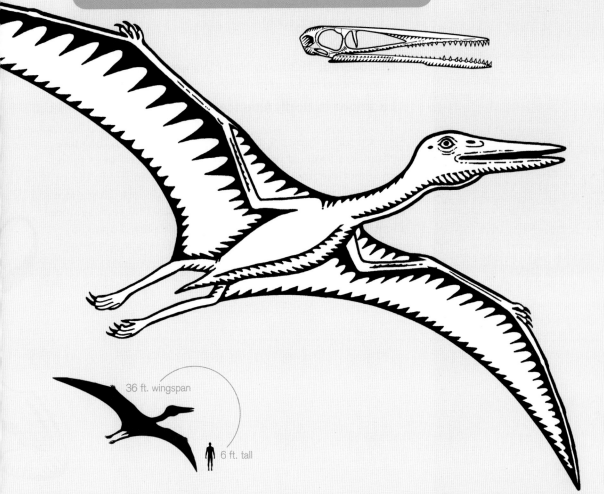

36 ft. wingspan

6 ft. tall

Smilodon

(Smile-oh-dawn)

Type of Prehistoric Animal: Saber-toothed cat

Meaning of Name: "Tooth shaped like double-edged knife"

Maximum Size: 9 feet long

Lived: 250,000 years ago to 10,000 years ago (Pleistocene Epoch)

Diet: Meat

Discovered: 1830s, by Peter Wilhelm Lund; scientifically described by Lund in 1842

Locations in North America: Widespread in North America

Smilodon—also known as the saber-toothed tiger—is the most well-known fossil cat in the world. Its remains have been found throughout the Americas and are especially abundant in the La Brea Tar Pits (see page 142). It appears that *Smilodon* was most successful during the late Pleistocene (from around 120,000 years ago until about 10,000 years ago), when it apparently preyed upon all manner of large animals, from condors to mammoths. Toward the end of this period, it increasingly began to run out of prey options, driving it to extinction.

Fun Facts:

Although often referred to as a "saber-toothed tiger" because of their astounding canine teeth, *Smilodon* is actually not all that closely related to tigers.

Smilodon's reliance on large prey animals, such as camels, may have caused its demise; at the end of the Ice Age most of these animals went extinct, and so too did *Smilodon*.

Widespread in North America

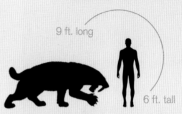

9 ft. long

6 ft. tall

Stylemys

(Sty-lem-ees)

Type of Prehistoric Animal: Giant tortoise

Meaning of Name: "Pillar turtle"

Maximum Size: Perhaps 6 feet long

Lived: 36–30 million years ago
(Eocene and Oligocene epochs)

Diet: Plants

Discovered: 1851, by Joseph Leidy

Locations in North America: NE, SD, WY, Saskatchewan

Some 35 million years ago, the giant tortoise *Stylemys* lived in the area now known as the Badlands of South Dakota and Nebraska. At that time, the environment was more subtropical and supported a variety of plants that were well suited to the *Stylemys's* diet and its primitive jaw muscles, which were far less sophisticated that those found in modern-day tortoises.

 Fun Facts:

The largest *Stylemys* tortoises may have reached lengths of up to six feet.

Fossils found in these states/provinces

6 ft. long

6 ft. tall

Recommended Reading

Bakker, Robert T. *The Dinosaur Heresies: New Theories Unlocking the Mystery of the Dinosaurs and Their Extinction.* Zebra: 1986.

Currie, Philip J. and Kevin Padian. *Encyclopedia of Dinosaurs.* Academic Press: 1997.

Discovery Channel Staff. *Discovery Dinopedia: The Complete Guide to Everything Dinosaur.* The Discovery Channel: 2014.

Dixon, Dougal. *The Complete Illustrated Encyclopedia Of Dinosaurs & Prehistoric Creatures: The Ultimate Illustrated Reference.* Southwater: 2014.

Dixon, Dougal and Andrew Robinson. *Illustrated Dinosaur Encyclopedia.* Gallery Books: 1991.

Dixon, Dougal and Barry Cox. *Macmillan Illustrated Encyclopedia of Dinosaurs and Prehistoric Animals: A Visual Who's Who of Prehistoric Life.* Macmillan: 1988.

Holtz, Jr. Thomas R. and Luis V. Rey. *Dinosaurs: The Most Complete, Up-to-Date Encyclopedia for Dinosaur Lovers of All Ages.* Random House: 2007.

Holtz, Jr. Thomas R. and Michael-Brett Surman. *Jurassic World Dinosaur Field Guide.* Random House for Young Readers: 2015.

Horner, John and James Gorman. *Digging Dinosaurs: The Search That Unraveled the Mystery of Baby Dinosaurs.* Perennial Library: 1988.

Horner, John and James Gorman. *How to Build a Dinosaur: The New Science of Reverse Evolution.* Plume: 2010.

Lambert, David. *Dinosaur Data Book: The Definitive, Fully Illustrated Encyclopedia of Dinosaurs.* Avon Books: 1990.

Lindsay, William. *Prehistoric Life: The Definitive Visual History of Life on Earth.* Dorling Kindersley: 2012.

Lockley, Martin. *Tracking Dinosaurs: A New Look at an Ancient World.* Cambridge University Press: 1991.

Lockley, Martin and Adrian P. Hunt. *Dinosaur Tracks of Western North America.* Columbia University Press: 1999.

Norman, David. *The Illustrated Encyclopedia of Dinosaurs.* Gramercy: 1988.

Parker, Steve. *Dinosaurus: The Complete Guide to Dinosaurs.* Firefly Books: 2009.

Paul, Gregory S. *The Princeton Field Guide to Dinosaurs.* Princeton University Press: 2010.

Paul, Gregory S. *The Scientific American Book of Dinosaurs.* Scientific American: 2000.

Pim, Keiron and Jack Horner. *Dinosaurs, The Grand Tour: Everything Worth Knowing About Dinosaurs from Aardonyx to Zuniceratops.* The Experiment Press: 2014.

Prothero, Donald R. *The Story of Life in 25 Fossils: Tales of Intrepid Fossil Hunters and the Wonders of Evolution.* Columbia University Press: 2015.

Sampson, Scott D. and Philip Currie. *Dinosaur Odyssey: Fossil Threads in the Web of Life.* University of California Press: 2011.

Turner, Alan and Mauricio Anton. *National Geographic Prehistoric Mammals.* National Geographic Press: 2004.

Museums Not to Miss

Alabama
McWane Science Center
Birmingham, Alabama
www.mcwane.org

Alaska
Alaska Museum of Science and Nature
Anchorage, Alaska
www.alaskamuseum.org

Arizona
Arizona Museum of Natural History
Mesa, Arizona
http://azmnh.org/

Yavapai Geology Museum
Grand Canyon Village, Arizona
www.nps.gov/grca

California
Los Angeles County Museum of Natural History
Los Angeles, California
www.nhm.org

San Diego Natural History Museum
San Diego, California
www.sdnhm.org

Canada
Royal Tyrrell Museum
Drumheller, Alberta, Canada
www.tyrrellmuseum.com

Colorado
Dinosaur Journey
Fruita, Colorado
www.museumofwesternco.com/visit/dinosaur-journey/

Museum of Natural History at the University of Colorado at Boulder
Boulder, Denver
cumuseum.colorado.edu

Rocky Mountain Dinosaur Resource Center
Woodland Park, Colorado
www.rmdrc.com

Connecticut
Connecticut Science Center
Hartford, Connecticut
www.ctsciencecenter.org

Dinosaur Place
Montville, Connecticut
http://naturesartvillage.com/thedinosaurplace/

Dinosaur State Park
Rocky Hill, Connecticut
www.dinosaurstatepark.org

Peabody Museum of Natural History
New Haven, Connecticut
http://peabody.yale.edu/

Delaware
Museum of Natural History
Wilmington, Delaware
www.delmnh.org

Florida
Florida Museum of Natural History
Gainesville, Florida
www.flmnh.ufl.edu

Georgia
Museum of Natural History
Athens, Georgia
http://naturalhistory.uga.edu

Idaho
Idaho Museum of Natural History
Pocatello, Idaho
http://imnh.isu.edu/home/

Illinois
Field Museum
Chicago, Illinois
www.fieldmuseum.org

Indiana
Indiana State Museum
Indianapolis, Indiana
www.indianamuseum.org

Iowa
University Iowa Museum of Natural History
Iowa City, Iowa
http://mnh.uiowa.edu/

Kansas

The University of Kentucky Biodiversity Institute and Museum of Natural History
Lawrence, Kansas
www.naturalhistory.ku.edu/

Louisiana

Lafayette Science Museum
Lafayette, Louisiana
www.lafayettesciencemuseum.org/

Louisiana State Museum of Natural Science
Baton Rouge, Louisiana
sites01.lsu.edu/wp/mns/

Museum of Natural History
Monroe, Louisiana
(University of Louisiana at Monroe)
www.ulm.edu/mnh/

Prehistoric Park
Henderson, Louisiana
www.prehistoric-park.com/

Maine

Dorr Museum of Natural History
Bar Harbor, Maine
www.coa.edu/html/museum.htm

Maryland

Maryland Science Center
Baltimore, Maryland
www.mdsci.org

Massachusetts

Museum of Science
Boston, Massachusetts
www.mos.org

Michigan

University of Michigan Museum of Natural History
Ann Arbor, Michigan
www.lsa.umich.edu/ummnh

Minnesota

Science Museum of Minnesota
St. Paul, Minnesota
www.smm.org

Mississippi

Mississippi Museum of Natural Science
Jackson, Mississippi
www.mdwfp.com

Missouri

Bollinger Museum of Natural History
Marble Hill, Missouri
www.bcmnh.org

Montana

Great Plains Dinosaur Museum
Malta, Montana
www.greatplainsdinosaurs.org

Museum of the Rockies
Bozeman, Montana
www.museumoftherockies.org

Two Medicine Dinosaur Center
Bynum, Montana
www.tmdinosaurcenter.org

Nebraska

University of Nebraska State Museum
Lincoln, Nebraska
www.museum.unl.edu

Nevada

Las Vegas Natural History Museum
Las Vegas, Nevada
www.lvnhm.org

New Jersey

Field Station: Dinosaurs
Secaucus, New Jersey
www.fieldstationdinosaurs.com

Haddonfield Dinosaur Information Center
Haddonfield, New Jersey
www.hadrosaurus.com

New Mexico

Mesalands Museum
Tucumcari, New Mexico
www.mesalands.edu/
community/dinosaur-museum

New Mexico Museum of Natural History
Albuquerque, New Mexico
www.nmnaturalhistory.org

New York
American Museum of
Natural History
New York, New York
www.amnh.org

North Carolina
Museum of Life and Science
Durham, North Carolina
http://lifeandscience.org/

Ohio
Cincinnati Museum Center
Cincinnati, Ohio
www.cincymuseum.org

Cleveland Museum of
Natural History
Cleveland, Ohio
www.cmnh.org

Oklahoma
Museum of the Red River
Idabel, Oklahoma
www.museumoftheredriver.org

Pennsylvania
The Academy of Natural
Sciences at Drexel University
Philadelphia, Pennsylvania
www.ansp.org/visit/exhibits/
dinosaur-hall

South Carolina
Charleston Museum
Charleston, South Carolina
www.charlestonmuseum.org

South Dakota
Black Hills Institute of
Geological Research
Hill City, South Dakota
www.bhigr.com

Journey Museum
Rapid City, South Dakota
http://journeymuseum.org/

South Dakota School of
Mines Museum of Geology
Rapid City, South Dakota
www.sdsmt.edu/Academics/
Museum-of-Geology/Home

Tennessee
East Tennessee University
and General Shale Natural
History Museum
Gray, Tennessee
www.etsu.edu/naturalhistory
museum

Texas
Dinosaur Park
Cedar Creek, Texas
www.thedinopark.com

Perot Museum of
Nature and Science
Dallas, Texas
www.perotmuseum.org

Utah
Dinosaur National Monument
Jensen, Utah
www.nps.gov/dino/index.htm

Museum of Ancient Life
Lehi, Utah
hwww.thanksgivingpoint.org/visit/
museumofancientlife

Natural History Museum
of Utah
Salt Lake City, Utah
https://nhmu.utah.edu/

Ogden Eccles Dinosaur Park
Ogden, Utah
www.dinosaurpark.org

Utah Field House of
Natural History
Vernal, Utah
http://stateparks.utah.gov/parks/
utah-field-house/

Virginia
Virginia Living Museum
Newport News, Virginia
https://thevlm.org/

Washington
Burke Museum
Seattle, Washington
www.burkemuseum.org

Washington, D.C.
Smithsonian Institution
National Museum of
Natural History
Washington, District of Columbia
www.mnh.si.edu

West Virginia
Virginia Museum of
Natural History
Martinsville, West Virginia
www.vmnh.net

Wisconsin
Dinosaur Discovery Museum
Kenosha, Wisconsin
www.kenosha.org/wp–dinosaur

Wyoming
State Museum
Cheyenne, Wyoming
www.wyomuseum.state.wy.us

Western Wyoming Natural
History Museum
Sweet Water County, Wyoming
www.westernwyoming.edu/about/
visit/dinosaurs.html

Wyoming Dinosaur Center
Thermopolis, Wyoming
www.wyodino.org

Glossary

Ankylosaur The name given to a clade of ornithischian dinosaurs that share bone structure and characteristics with *Ankylosaurus*, the predominant member of the group. Many of the four-legged, armored dinosaurs are members of this group.

Brachiosaur/Brachiosaurid One of a group of large, quadruped, herbivorous dinosaurs that share characteristics with *Brachiosaurus*, such as large body, long neck and tail, and forelimbs larger than hind.

Camarasaur/Camarasaurid The name given to a group of dinosaurs that share bone structure and characteristics with *Camarasaurus*.

Carnosaur Originally a name given to a large group of theropod dinosaurs that share characteristics with *Allosaurus*. However, it has been redefined and many of the original members have been assigned to other groups—such as the tyrannosaurs.

Ceratopsid A large and diverse group of quadruped, herbivorous dinosaurs known primarily for their remarkable, often ornate, frills and facial horns. Members include *Triceratops* and *Styracosaurus*.

Coelophysid/Coelophysidae A family of early theropod dinosaurs that shared characteristics with *Coelophysis*.

Diplodocid A member of a group of dinosaurs that share bone structure and characteristics with *Diplodocus*.

Dromaeosaur/Dromaeosaurid/Dromaeosauridae A family of small, often feathered, carnivorous dinosaurs that share bone structure and characteristics with *Dromaeosaurus*.

Hadrosaur The name given to a group of dinosaurs that share bone structure and characteristics with *Hadrosaurus*.

Hypsilophodont A group of small, herbivorous, bipedal dinosaurs up to about six feet long.

Ornithischia One of the major dinosaur divisions, characterized by their "bird-hipped" pelvic bone structure. Ironically, birds did not descend from ornithischians. Rather, they originated in the other major dinosaur group—the saurischia—as part of the theropods.

Ornithomimosaur The name given to a group of dinosaurs that share bone structure and characteristics with *Ornithomimosaurus*.

Osteoderm Bony growths that occur scattered in the skin of some animals, including many dinosaurus, as well as alligators and crocodiles.

Pachycephalosaur A clade of bipedal, ornithischian dinosaurs that share characteristics with the primary genus *Pachycephalosaurus*.

Paleontology The study of fossils and the prehistory of Earth.

Pathology Evidence of injury or disease. Paleopathology especially references abnormal bones or bone growth.

Saurischia One of the major, if informal, dinosaur divisions, characterized by their "lizard-hipped" pelvic bone structure.

Sauropod A distinct group of saurischian dinosaurs characterized by long necks and tails.

Stegosaur/Stegosaurid A group of quadruped, herbivorous, ornithischian dinosaurs that had characteristics in common with *Stegosaurus*. Most had armor along their backs.

Theropod A major group of saurischian dinosaurs, primarily carnivorous (although some are herbivorous) and almost always bipedal. Birds are descendants of this group.

Tracks/Trackways Preserved footprints of animals. Study of such fossils is called paleoichnology.

Tyrannosaur The name given to a group of bipedal, theropod dinosaurs that share structure and characteristics with *Tyrannosaurus*.

About the Authors

Jon Kramer

By the time he was four, Jon was digging fossils from Calvert Cliffs along Chesapeake Bay, unearthing fossil shark teeth from the famous Miocene sediments. His parents encouraged his passions as he was raised in the family rock and gem business. Jon is a graduate of the University of Maryland, where he founded the Geology Club and led field trips across the US in search of fossils. As an intern at the Vertebrate Paleontology Lab at the Smithsonian Institution, Jon helped prepare and assemble dinosaurs and fossil mammals for display in the exhibit halls. While there he developed relationships with leading paleontologists around the world and with many has authored numerous academic papers on a variety of fossil subjects.

Jon founded Potomac Museum Group as a natural outgrowth of his museum experience and business background. During its 30-year heyday PMG dug fossils around the world and created traveling educational exhibits which toured North America for two decades. PMG also maintained a dinosaur dig site in Wyoming for nearly ten years starting in the late 1980s.

These days Jon continues his paleontological passion, digging fossils and supporting research. Jon and his wife Julie regularly donate specimens to museums, universities, schools, and education groups.

Julie Martinez

Julie's appreciation for nature started in childhood and has grown throughout her life. She maintains extensive collections of insects, plants, rocks, shells, and fossils from around the world.

Julie graduated from the University of Wisconsin, Stevens Point with a degree in Fine Arts and Biology. For five years she worked at the University of Minnesota creating illustrations for the medical field. In the late 1980s she began a freelance career as a scientific illustrator working with studios, museums, universities, and publishing companies. Julie's work is featured in many textbooks, journals and museum exhibits throughout North America. She was commissioned by Potomac Museum Group to supply all of the detailed scientific illustration for its exhibits, amounting to hundreds of full-color panels in painstaking detail.

Julie travels extensively to learn more about her subjects, exploring rain forests and deserts alike, often with her husband, Jon. Both of them continue to excavate fossils, support research, and donate to science.

Vernon Morris

Early in his life Vern learned the value of nature and the Great Spirit through elders of his Native American Anishinaabe tribe. He pursued nature interests throughout his life via artistic expression and schooled in commercial illustration and design at the University of Minnesota.

In the 1980s Vern's art came to the attention of Potomac Museum Group where he eventually became the staff muralist for all of PMG's traveling exhibits. During his tenure at PMG he painted many iconic scenes, including Ice Age mammoths on the frozen tundra and herds of dinosaurs crossing mid-continental mudflats of the Jurassic. Vern is also adept at sculpture, recreating lifelike dinosaurs and fossil mammals alike.

Vern immerses himself in learning about his subjects—traveling to museums and excavation sites and interviewing researchers. As a result, Vern has been an invaluable asset in most of PMG's fossil expeditions. He continues to paint prehistoric scenes, as well as excavate fossils and support research, often accompanying Jon and Julie on expeditions out West.